Nigel Davies was born in 1920 and educated at Eton. He was Conservative MP for Epping from 1951, where he succeeded to part of Winston Churchill's wartime constituency. In 1962 he settled in Mexico City, where he studied at the National University of Mexico, and he took his doctorate in archaeology at London University. He now devotes himself to writing and lecturing on ancient America, and he is the author of *The Aztecs*, *The Toltecs*, *The Toltec Heritage*, *Voyagers to the New World: Fact and Fantasy*, *Human Sacrifice*, *The Rampant God*, *The Aztec Empire*, *The Ancient Kingdoms of Mexico* (also published by Penguin) and *The Incas*. In 1980 the President of Mexico awarded Nigel Davies the prestigious order of the Aztec Eagle for his contribution to Mexican culture.

NIGEL DAVIES

———

THE ANCIENT KINGDOMS
OF PERU

PENGUIN BOOKS

PENGUIN BOOKS

Published by the Penguin Group
Penguin Books Ltd, 80 Strand, London WC2R 0RL, England
Penguin Putnam Inc., 375 Hudson Street, New York, New York 10014, USA
Penguin Books Australia Ltd, 250 Camberwell Road, Camberwell, Victoria 3124, Australia
Penguin Books Canada Ltd, 10 Alcorn Avenue, Toronto, Ontario, Canada M4V 3B2
Penguin Books India (P) Ltd, 11 Community Centre, Panchsheel Park, New Delhi – 110 017, India
Penguin Books (NZ) Ltd, Cnr Rosedale and Airborne Roads, Albany, Auckland, New Zealand
Penguin Books (South Africa) (Pty) Ltd, 24 Sturdee Avenue, Rosebank 2196, South Africa

Penguin Books Ltd, Registered Offices: 80 Strand, London WC2R 0RL, England

www.penguin.com

Frst published 1997
10

Set in 10/12pt Monotype Bembo
Typeset by Rowland Phototypesetting Ltd, Bury St Edmunds, Suffolk
Printed in England by Clays Ltd, St Ives plc

CONTENTS

LIST OF FIGURES

LIST OF MAPS

LIST OF ILLUSTRATIONS

In a previous book on the Inca Empire I was solely concerned with the last 150 years before the Spanish Conquest in A D 1532. But since the Incas themselves had no writing system, most of the relevant data are derived from the records, not of Incas, but of Spaniards. Some of these took part in the Conquest, while others obtained certain information from Inca nobles, mainly resident in Cuzco. In recent decades these accounts have been analysed and reinterpreted by modern scholars.

Certain legends concerning pre-Inca civilizations also survive, such as king-lists for the realm of Chimor, that preceded the rise of the Incas. However, our knowledge of pre-Inca Peru derives basically from the findings of archaeologists.

In the last few decades Peru and the Andean region in general have been fortunate in their ability to attract many distinguished scholars, not only from Peru but from many lands, who have been able to unearth a wealth of new data on a long series of ancient Andean cultures. These were not necessarily 'kingdoms' in the accepted sense of the word; as we shall see, none ever came to dominate the whole of Peru, let alone its nearest neighbours. Their achievements have been amply documented in a copious range of publications.

Much of this book is devoted to the more outstanding of these pre-Inca cultures. Some were basically centred inland, like the Incas themselves, in the high Andean region. The cultures of the first and second millennia B C, of which our knowledge has now been vastly increased, were at least partly maritime, while the Moche, who flourished in the first six centuries A D, were mainly confined to coastal Peru. Recent finds have also made spectacular contributions to our knowledge of the Moche period. After the Moche decline, in what is known as the Middle Period, the principal centres of power were based inland: on the one hand Huari and nearby sites, and on the other Tiahuanaco on the Bolivian side of Lake Titicaca.

Following the demise of Huari, by far the largest centre of power was once more a coastal civilization, that of Chimor, which occupied an extensive territory, later also to be conquered by the Incas.

CHAPTER ONE

THE BIRTH OF CIVILIZATION

A Land of Contrasts

Peru is a land of sharp contrasts. From north to south a flat strip of desert borders the Pacific Ocean, so arid that it supports no visible form of plant life. However, this wasteland is intersected by many rivers whose green and fertile valleys present a marked contrast to the long stretches of desert sand. The Pacific Ocean itself, due to the Humboldt Current, is much colder on the coast of Peru than most waters of comparable latitudes in other parts of the world; as a result, though rainfall is a scant phenomenon, the sky is at times cloudy, particularly in the vicinity of the present-day capital, Lima, where a strong sun beats on the cold sea and causes vapour to rise and form clouds.

In marked contrast to the coastal strip, a few miles to the east rises the majestic range of the Andes that stretches southwards into Chile. Part of this central area of Peru is uncultivable, since it consists of rocky, snow-clad peaks. However, between these mountains, which in effect form two parallel ranges, lie many fertile valleys; located at altitudes of between 2500 and 3500 metres, these enjoy a regular rainfall during the summer months and support a wide range of plant and animal life. As an example, one may cite the Valley of Cuzco, the future Inca capital, with an average elevation of 3500 metres; among the highest and most exotic valleys, situated at the south-eastern extremity of Peru, is the basin in which lies Lake Titicaca, the highest navigable water in the world; as we shall later see, this region played an important role in the history of ancient times.

Beyond the Andes lies a third region which embraces over half of the total area of modern Peru. Known as the *montañas*, it consists of lush lowlands, whose northern extremity forms part of the great basin of the Amazon River. This region was the home of peoples whose contacts with the more advanced cultures of the Andean valleys were somewhat limited, though Inca sources mention various rather inconclusive military campaigns against lowland tribes.

The date of the arrival of human beings in Peru and its neighbours remains somewhat controversial. Scholars now generally agree that a human presence in the Andean region occurred before 9000 BC; earlier radiocarbon dates, such as those of Richard MacNeish, indicating a human occupation of the Valley of Ayacucho before 20,000 BC, are not universally accepted. These early Peruvians were clearly descended from small groups of people who had first colonized the New World after crossing from Asia in the region of the Bering Strait, at a time when a land bridge between Asia and America still existed; at least one of these groups eventually crossed the Isthmus of Panama and thereby became the ancestors of the Andean peoples.

These early settlers followed the fairly typical pattern of hunter-gatherers. For instance, Michael Moseley writes of sites belonging to what is known as the Paiján tradition, yielding radiocarbon dates of before 8000 BC. Finds have been made of stone quarries and lithic workshops at La Cumbre on the north side of the Río Moche Valley, a region which, as we shall later see, played a major role in the history of ancient Peru. Places located at higher altitudes seem to have been also occupied at this time; for instance, one may cite the excavations of Pachamachay Cave, situated inland at an elevation of 4300 metres and occupied by hunter-gatherers who preyed upon the various cameloid species which abounded in the region.

These hunter-gatherers attained the next step on the road to civilization, the cultivation of plants, both for food as well as for the making of mats and containers. Dates of 8000 BC exist both for Guitarrero Cave, relatively near the coast, and for the Tres Ventanas Caves, situated further inland at an altitude of 3900 metres; fragments of cultivated gourd have been found of comparable antiquity in the Ayacucho region.

As early as about 6000 BC, evidence survives of small villages on the northern coast of Peru, and at one site, Nanchoc, twin mounds have been excavated that appear to constitute a primitive form of ceremonial construction. For truly monumental architecture, generally taken to

Figure 1 Primitive Dwelling, Approximately 3000 BC

indicate the presence of a more complex society, we have radiocarbon dates of between 2900 and 2700 BC for the site of Aspero, situated on the coast to the north of Lima; a sample from a nearby platform mound of the Huaca de los Idolos provided a date of 3000 BC.

Unexpected Discoveries

Aspero, first taken to consist merely of natural mounds, was first excavated in 1941 by Gordon Willey and John Corbett. As they were fully aware, the presence of some form of pottery was then regarded as a universal characteristic of even the earliest monumental architecture throughout the world. Undeterred by the apparent lack of ceramics at Aspero, they therefore proceeded to offer a comparatively late date for the site, based on pottery none of which was found at Aspero itself, but in a nearby cemetery!

Only about two decades later was the wholly astonishing fact reluctantly accepted that not only did Aspero indeed have no pottery, but that it formed part of an extensive architectural pattern; this included a number of monumental preceramic sites, such as El Paraiso in the Río Chillon Valley, and above all the highland site of Kotosh, much further inland, where archaeologists of the University of Tokyo

3

investigated large structures of many kinds in different layers, all of which lacked pottery. These preceramic sites of Peru are among the oldest forms of monumental architecture in the New World; the earliest are contemporary with the great pyramids of the Old Kingdom in Egypt!

To take one example of this period, major excavations at Aspero revealed a series of mounds that were not simply earthen platforms, but whose successive phases consisted of walled rooms. These stone walls were plastered and some were painted red or yellow. In the Huaca de los Idolos, the largest platform mound at Aspero, an elaborate pattern of rooms survives, with walls that contained niches. In the Huaca de los Sacrificios at Aspero, a ceremonial burial of an infant was found, wrapped in textiles and surrounded by grave goods; some were made of exotic materials such as coloured feathers, stone beads and even spondylus shells that must have been brought from Ecuador.

One outstanding characteristic of these ruins that continued into the subsequent ceramic phase, is the presence of sunken courts, particularly in sites on the coast. In the more typical examples of such sites an independent rectangular platform is built with stairs that lead down to a circular court, generally situated within a rectangular forecourt. For instance, at Salinas de Chao, a large site on the shoreline of the Río Chao Valley, a terraced platform forty metres wide had three flights of stairs that led to a circular plaza with painted walls; an estimated 100,000 tons of stones were used in its construction. The principal form of visual art in these preceramic sites was that of cotton textiles. Motifs included two-headed snakes and stylized birds that formed antecedents for art styles of later Peruvian cultures.

Another major preceramic site is the highland settlement of La Galgada, where some of the earliest vestiges of irrigation were found. While grave goods in the form of pottery are obviously lacking, elaborate burials contain beaded necklaces, and many individuals were already buried with textiles and cotton bags with complex designs. La Galgada had two major mounds; the larger of the two was over fifteen metres high; a succession of chambers with central firepits were built on the summit. Unlike other contemporary sites, archaeologists have located the remains of human dwellings in the vicinity; fifty rustic buildings are recognizable as houses rather than temples.

During the preceramic phase the first so-called U-shaped design of ceremonial buildings also appeared. As an example, one may cite the layout of El Paraiso, near the mouth of the Río Chillon; the largest of all the preceramic sites, it foreshadows the subsequent U-shaped complexes of the second millennium.

Further Surprises

What is currently called the Initial Period, traditionally begins not with the dates of the great preceramic sites named above, but with later dates that derive from the first introduction of pottery in about 1800 BC.

The unearthing of sites built long before this date had been quite unexpected; at the time of the 1941 excavations at Aspero, the Peruvian archaeologist Julio Tello continued to advance the notion that this and other sites were 'Chavinoid', and somehow influenced by the great centre of Chavin, still then held to be the oldest of all the known sites of Peru, serving as the cultural inspiration of all early monuments.

Since Chavin was then currently regarded as the very first civilization in Peru, its people were compared with the Sumerians of Mesopotamia or the Olmecs in Mexico! John Rowe as late as 1962 defined the Early Horizon as beginning with the introduction of Chavin influence into Ica, a small valley on the south coast of Peru.

Having drawn such seemingly obvious conclusions, arising from studies of other early civilizations, archaeologists were confronted with yet another surprise, which conclusively reversed their original findings. On the basis of radiocarbon dating, it eventually became clear that Chavin, far from being the first of these early Peruvian cultures, is the last, and dates from about 800 BC, or about 1000 years later than the earliest Peruvian pottery.

Traditionally regarded as the originator of early Peruvian fine arts and monumental architecture, Chavin is now seen as the successor rather than the precursor of the earlier ceremonial centres basic to Andean civilization. Moreover, it is now in effect realized that Chavin, which is defined as belonging to the Early Horizon, was preceded by not one but two previous cultural phases: first by the preceramic era, including centres that date from as early as 3000 BC, and thereafter by

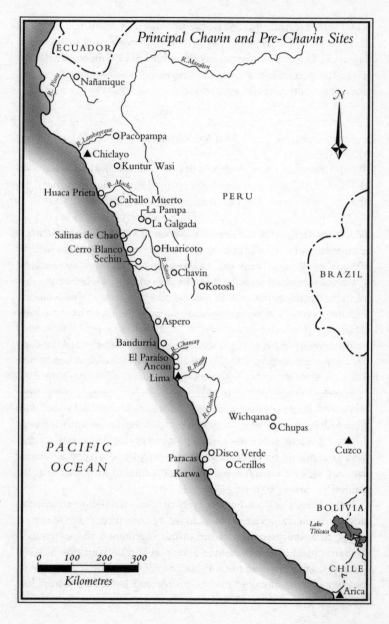

Principal Chavin and Pre-Chavin Sites

ECUADOR

R. Piura

R. Marañón

Nañanique

PERU

R. Lambayeque

Pacopampa

▲ Chiclayo

Kuntur Wasi

R. Moche

Huaca Prieta

Caballo Muerto

La Pampa

La Galgada

Salinas de Chao

Cerro Blanco

Huaricoto

Sechin

R. Santa

Chavin

BRAZIL

Kotosh

Aspero

Bandurria

R. Chancay

El Paraiso

Ancon

R. Rimac

Lima ▲

R. Chincha

Wichqana

Chupas

PACIFIC
OCEAN

Cuzco ▲

Paracas

Disco Verde

Cerillos

Karwa

BOLIVIA

*Lake
Titicaca*

N

0   100   200   300

CHILE

Kilometres

Arica ▲

a second era, now generally termed the Initial Period, which lasted from about 1800 to 800 BC. To this second phase many sites belong which already produced pottery and in which two forms of ceremonial architecture continued to prevail, the circular sunken courts and the U-shaped mound complexes. The discovery of the fact that the imposing site of Chavin de Huantar, far from being the originator of art and architecture in Peru, dates from after, not before, many of the early ceremonial centres, has revolutionized our notions as to the origins of Andean civilization.

The Initial Period

To this era, defined as beginning in about 1800 BC, belongs a plethora of imposing sites; it is marked not only by the production of the earliest ceramics but by new farming techniques, in particular the development of irrigation, which led to the establishment of larger settlements in the coastal desert, and to the growth of more complex centres of population, both on the coast and in the highlands, where monumental architecture became quite widespread.

Among the most impressive examples of the many sites of the Initial Period are those of the Sechin complex in the Río Casma Valley. Of these, Cerro Sechin is probably the best known. During the latter part of the Initial Period this site covered five hectares. Consisting basically of a three-tiered stepped platform, its outer wall was adorned with nearly 400 stone carvings. To cite Richard Burger's description, these stone sculptures, made from granite blocks quarried from a nearby hill, were arranged in the platform wall to portray a single scene, in which two columns of warriors approach each other from opposing sides amidst the carnage of their adversaries.

The figures depicted on the sculptured stones represent humans rather than animals. Victorious warriors are shown only on the largest stones, arrayed in flowing loincloths. More frequent is the portrayal of the defeated, always naked; nude bodies are shown with eyes bulging and torsos often sliced in two. About 70 per cent of the carvings show decapitated heads, usually with eyes closed, ready to be used as trophies. Burger suggests that Cerro Sechin, sometimes interpreted as a kind of war memorial, is simply another example of ceremonial architecture decorated with religious themes; perhaps they represent some mythical battle won by ancestral heroes.

The largest of the sites of the Casma region is Sechin Alto, only two kilometres distant from Cerro Sechin. The principal mound, measuring 250 by 300 metres at its base, is probably the largest single building constructed in the New World during the second millennium BC, though due to much looting it is less well preserved than Cerro Sechin. It formed part of a large ceremonial complex; four huge rectangular plazas stretch out from the central mound, three of which have sunken circular courts in their centre.

The Sechin complex, a striking example of building during the Initial Period, is but one of a large number of surviving monuments of that epoch, both on the coast and inland. Not only were large sites situated further to the north, such as Huaca de los Reyes, located twenty-five kilometres inland; others exist in the vicinity of Lima, for instance La Florida, which dates from about 1710 BC and is estimated to have required some seven million man days to construct. Highland sites of the Initial Period survive as far distant as Chiripa on the shore of Lake Titicaca.

The more northerly sites of this period, such as Huaca de los Reyes, share a common religious tradition of art and architecture known as Cupisnique, notable for its pottery and above all for its peculiar adobe sculptured figures; to cite one example, when the site of Huaca de los Reyes was excavated, fine adobe sculptures came to light, including giant three-dimensional feline heads with snarling faces and huge clenched teeth.

Chavin

The phase defined as the Initial Period drew to an end in about 800 BC. During the following period, known as the Early Horizon, inland sites, particularly Chavin, rose to prominence. Chavin de Huantar, situated to the north-west of Kotosh, is located at an altitude of 3150 metres; it stands roughly halfway between the Pacific Ocean and the tropical forest. According to Richard Burger, who has written at length

Figure 2 Stone Warriors from Cerro Sechin

on Chavin, it was founded in about 900 BC. The rise of this very important site coincides with a gradual collapse of the U-shaped centres of the coast, a process which was more or less completed by 500 BC.

In the earlier Chavin period, known as the Urabarriu phase, estimated to have lasted until about 500 BC, the Chavin Old Temple was built. To the final phase, known as Janabarriu, which ended in around 200 BC, belongs the completion of the New Temple. By this time the population of Chavin had greatly expanded and its pottery was the object of long-distance exchange.

The quality and sophistication of the metallurgy, textiles and ceramics, found both in the site itself and in an extensive region where Chavin influence is present, suggest that they were the work of specialized artists. Metallurgy was at that time in its infancy; small pieces of hammered copper sheet have been found at the site of Mina Perdida, probably made a little before 1000 BC. However, it now seems clear that the spread of Chavin culture, both on the coast and in the highlands, was far from universal. For instance, the Valley of Cuzco, the future Inca capital, is now seen as having had much stronger ties with fairly complex societies that were then developing around Lake Titicaca than with Chavin.

The earliest part of the Chavin complex, usually described as the Old Temple, was, like the centres already described above, a U-shaped platform enclosing a sunken circular courtyard. On the exterior stone walls at approximately ten metres from the ground stood a series of animal and human stone heads, displaying contorted features and crude fangs; their size is more than double that of ordinary human heads.

An unusual characteristic of this temple is the number of interior galleries, built at different levels and connected by stairways. In some galleries traces of slabs survive, decorated with incised and painted figures; others contained fine ceramics. At the point where the two arms of the lower gallery cross is an imposing stela, known as El Lanzón, thus named by the archaeologist Julio Tello. Because of its lance-like form, Burger considers that it represented the supreme deity of Chavin. Another gallery, known as the Gallery of Offerings, contains a remarkable collection of pottery, with motifs that recall Cupisnique models. Apart from their usage as storage space, it has been suggested that the galleries housed priests or initiates.

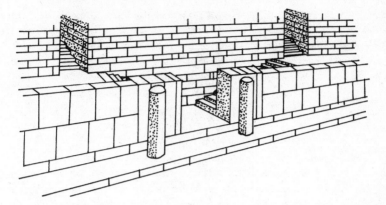

Figure 3 Details of Principal Façade of Chavin Temple

The Old Temple belongs to the early Urabarriu phase of the Chavin culture. Probably during the first part of the following phase, known as Chakinani, the construction of the New Temple began. This remodelling of the original structure transformed the right arm of the older U-shaped building into a massive pyramid; as a result of this reconstruction, the New Temple became part of a complex of large sunken rectangular courtyards. The New Temple represented the form of Chavin architecture that spread through much of the central Andes and even influenced the architecture of Tiahuanaco, situated on Lake Titicaca in Bolivia.

While, as we have seen, many of the principal sites of the Initial Period collapsed, the rise of Chavin in the Early Horizon was paralleled by other major centres; one may cite as an example Pacopampa, another inland site, lying to the north of Chavin, where a massive subterranean plaza contains carved columns and lintels typical of this period. At Kuntur Wasi, also situated to the north of Chavin in the Río Jequetepeque Valley, the staircases of the central plaza were decorated with stone carvings similar to those of Chavin itself. Other sites, such as Kotosh, already prominent in the Initial Period, survived and new constructions were added that were reminiscent of the Chavin style.

Ever since the earliest studies of Chavin were made, its influence has been viewed as the expression of some kind of religious ideology. The

Figure 4 El Lanzón

famous Raimondi Stone found in the New Temple continues to reflect certain themes already present in the El Lanzón stone shaft of the Old Temple, including the fangs so typical of the Chavin deity. Such fangs are also a feature of the famous Tello Obelisk which represents a kind of supernatural cayman, though not all its traits are drawn from the cayman, an aquatic predator; the tail is not crocodilian but presents the features of an eagle or hawk. Along with the jaguar, not only the cayman but also the crested eagle and the serpent were among the most common themes in Chavin art.

The rather enigmatic Chavin religious cult, found in many regions, was originally thought to be centred upon a purely feline god. But this view has now been modified. The feline god was certainly important in Chavin cosmology, as depicted, for instance, on some of the sculptures

Figure 5 A Stone Feline from Chavin with Cylindric Jar on Its Back

of the Old Temple. A curious feature of Chavin religious imagery is the presence of lowland crops that cannot be grown at the altitude of Chavin, such as manioc, bottle gourd and hot peppers. This has given rise to suggestions that its first settlers had migrated to Chavin from the Amazon or Orinoco basins. Moreover, the development of the basic ideology of the Chavin period would be hard to define in precise terms, since certain art forms traditionally described as Chavinoid predate the earliest remains of the site of Chavin itself.

While the iconography of Chavin is unquestionably defined in the fine stonework in Chavin itself, there is no evidence that large stone objects were made for export. The extent of its influence can better be defined by the presence in other sites of Chavin ceramics and textiles, both utilitarian and religious.

The extensive spread of the Chavin cult is exemplified by the site of Karwa, whose cemetery, situated eight kilometres south of the Paracas Necropolis, was first discovered by looters. Over 200 fragments of decorated Chavin-style textiles were recovered, together with a small number of shards also associated with those textiles.

Spheres of Influence

On the basis of evidence now available, it must be admitted that Chavin cultural influence was less universal than Tello had originally proposed. For instance, the Chanapata culture, situated in the Valley of Cuzco, was one of many groups that also maintained strong links with the peoples of the Lake Titicaca basin, where complex societies were already developing. Impressive temples had been erected in this area before 600 BC, but their stone images were unrelated to Chavin art.

As Richard Burger points out, the centres of the Chavin horizon, their massive structures decorated with detailed stone sculptures, were the product of a complex society and a well-established system of social stratification. Specific elements of Chavin civilization can be traced back as far as the preceramic era.

In other respects Chavin inherited basic features of Andean culture, such as the role of textiles as the highest art form and the production of fine gold and silver objects. Many centuries later, as we shall see, the people of Moche revived Chavin motifs in their ceramics, while the people of Tiahuanaco began to worship a Staff God similar to the image on the Raimondi Stone, a deity whose cult was to become widespread throughout the Peruvian highlands.

CHAPTER TWO

MOCHE

Basic to the study of the Moche culture is some definition of the different phases of its development. A beginning in this respect was made as early as 1899 by Max Uhle, who excavated thirty-one grave lots from the pyramids in the Río Moche Valley, the site that had given its name to the whole culture, whose remains have since been found over a more extensive area. Moche was then divided into five phases, covering the first six centuries of the Christian era, proposed by Rafael Larco-Hoyle in 1948. His definition of their chronology was based on burials in various sites that embraced all these five phases, each of which displayed certain characteristics of its own.

A most unusual feature of Moche studies is the fact that the most spectacular vestiges, far from emerging at an early stage, were only discovered quite recently.

Not until 1987, some eighty-eight years after the first investigations of Max Uhle in the Río Moche Valley, were the most dazzling remains of the Moche culture revealed to the world, not initially by archaeologists but by robbers. As described by Sidney Kirkpatrick, the location of certain Moche tombs in the heart of Huaca Rajada, a pyramid complex near the village of Sipan, situated on the remote, sunbaked plains of Lambayeque, some 170 kilometres north of the Río Moche, remained a lost secret until a team of impoverished thieves penetrated one of these tombs on a cool, moonlit night in February 1987.

The most vivid account of how this tomb came to be opened was that of Ernil Bernal, an unemployed truck driver and the self-appointed spokesman for the looters. Ernil and his friends had carved a tunnel into the smallest of the three pyramids of Huaca Rajada. Their first

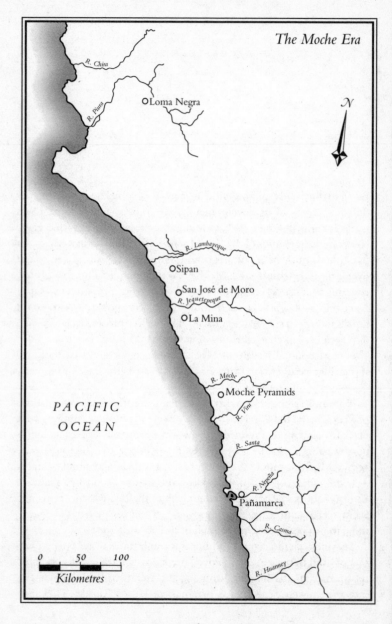

The Moche Era

N

R. Chira

R. Piura

○Loma Negra

R. Lambayeque

○Sipan

○San José de Moro

R. Jequetepeque

○La Mina

R. Moche

○Moche Pyramids

R. Viru

R. Santa

PACIFIC
OCEAN

R. Nepeña

○Pañamarca

R. Casma

0   50   100

Kilometres

R. Huarmey

find was a clutch of gold beads of a quality never unearthed in any other Moche site. In addition, construction techniques were visible in a roof above their heads of a kind that had never been found by professional investigators in sites looted long ago; at each level of penetration, the architecture of the pyramid changed.

In seeking an exit from the structure, Ernil's rod penetrated the floor of a room suspended above his tunnel and he unexpectedly found himself in an intact royal burial chamber that poured out its contents until he was buried up to his shoulders in a trove of priceless gold and silver ornaments, together with ancient carvings studded with precious stones.

But before presenting in more detail the story of what has emerged from Huaca Rajada, it may be more congruent first to record the results of earlier Moche research which, among other notable finds, yielded so many painted ceramic vases, which illustrated precisely the type of treasures finally uncovered in Huaca Rajada. The better-known Moche sites had been looted so long ago. Hence, no unviolated tomb of a Moche lord, containing the very kind of objects shown on these ceramics, had ever been excavated by archaeologists.

Moche Research

Records of anything resembling the culture of the Moche period were lacking in folk tradition of late pre-Conquest times. However, nebulous accounts apparently survived of coastal kingdoms that preceded the Chimu period, which began in about 700 AD and for which certain lists, including names of specific rulers, did survive, as we shall see in Chapter 5.

Among reports of such pre-Chimor coastal kingdoms the clearest is that of Bishop Bartolomé de las Casas, writing around 1550. He refers to an early period that lasted about five or six hundred years, during which many separate principalities thrived, some larger than others, but none of great size. The people of the coast, during this early period, reportedly used javelins in their wars, whereas the contemporary high-landers employed slings as their chief weapon of offence. The early rulers would build their palaces on hills or, if none were available, would cause their people to pile up vast mounds of earth in order to make an artificial eminence (a practice which, as we shall see, indeed prevailed during the period of which the mud-brick pyramids of the Río Moche Valley are among the most visible surviving evidence).

As related by the earliest investigators, at about the beginning of the Christian era, a culture began to develop which gradually became predominant in all the river valleys from the Río Piura southwards to the Río Huarney, a distance of over 500 kilometres, and which lasted until the eighth century AD. It was named Moche because the most conspicuous remains were found on that river and the division into five phases, Moche I to V, is in effect based on these remains. But while the Moche culture occupied a long coastline, its east–west extension was limited and Moche settlements are found only between the sea and the canyons that lead up to the high Andes, a distance of between sixty and eighty kilometres.

The vestiges of the first of the five phases, Moche I, correspond approximately to the beginning of the Christian era. The great pyramids of Cerro Blanco in the Río Moche Valley, representing the period Moche I to Moche IV, survived until shortly before AD 600, when they appear to have been struck by catastrophic floods and the site was abandoned after everything was buried by sand dunes, except for the two great pyramids still visible today. It is, however, important to stress that whereas research of Moche I to Moche IV was until quite recently concentrated on Cerro Blanco and nearby sites, it is now believed that even in these earlier phases the Moche civilization extended further north, up to the Río Lambayeque Valley, and even beyond.

Moreover, the final phase, Moche V, is to be found more in places further to the north, centred upon the important site of Pampa Grande, at the neck of the Río Lambayeque Valley, which survived until about AD 700. The ceramics of Moche V already exhibit some traits of the Huari culture that followed the demise of Moche. In other respects also the Moche V style differs markedly from that of the earlier phases.

Antecedents

The Moche culture of the northern coast of Peru had certain antecedents in the last two centuries before the birth of Christ, following the termination of the Cupisnique period. Of the first of these Moche predecessors, known as Salinar, a series of burials derive from a beach site located eleven kilometres north-west of the city of Trujillo; the site extends about four kilometres along the beach and up to one kilometre inland. New forms and features appear in Salinar pottery whose decoration consisted mainly of white painted bands or dots on a red paste. Use of copper was added to the earlier gold-working tradition. During the Salinar phase the area of cultivation in the Río Moche Valley was greatly enlarged. Another Salinar site, Cerro Arena, is also situated in the Río Moche Valley about ten kilometres inland; this ridgetop settlement has well-preserved domestic architecture and a few small temple mounds.

In the first century BC, Salinar was followed by another pre-Moche culture known as Gallinazo, which in effect overlaps with Moche I. Gallinazo architects already undertook impressive projects, including terraced platforms built at a fairly high level. A major Gallinazo site was situated on the west side of Cerro Blanco, where the great Moche pyramids were later to be built. The nature of this settlement is difficult to assess because of the subsequent Moche occupation. It is possible that the Moche Pyramid of the Moon may owe its origins to this period.

An important Gallinazo site was Cerro Orejas, also situated along the Río Moche Valley, somewhat further inland than Cerro Arena. The site is more than three kilometres in length and two large platforms of mud bricks survive, together with many rooms that served as domestic quarters. Irrigation, which may have begun even earlier, certainly existed in Gallinazo times, when large canals were constructed. Gallinazo produced impressive effigy pots of a type that became so typical of Moche, while its architectural concepts were also in effect the predecessors of those of Moche.

The Moche Mountains

The beginning of the first century AD marked the outset of the Moche era, with its grandiose buildings of mud brick.

At the site of Cerro Blanco, situated to the south of the Río Moche, somewhat nearer to the sea than Cerro Orejas, was erected the Pyramid of the Sun, the largest of the Moche pyramids and one of the biggest monuments ever constructed in pre-Hispanic America; it covers more than five hectares at its base and rises to a height of forty-one metres. During the seventeenth century looters diverted waters from the Río Moche in an attempt to undercut the Pyramid of the Sun and thus facilitate the removal of its contents at every level; as a result, about two-thirds of the platform was destroyed and the western side was washed away. Written evidence survives of the impressive loot extracted at that time. From the great gap in the structure created by this flooding it can be seen that construction probably began in phase I of the Moche style and continued until the end of phase IV.

At a distance of about 500 metres to the south of the Pyramid of the Sun is a monument known as the Pyramid of the Moon. It differs from the Pyramid of the Sun, since it is really a complex of three platforms, formerly enclosed by high adobe walls. The smallest of these platforms was built at the outset of the Moche era, whereas the largest was not erected until the Moche III stage. Unlike the Pyramid of the Sun, the walls of the Pyramid of the Moon were adorned with impressive murals.

These two great monuments formed part of a large urban complex filled with fine adobe residences for the ruling class, together with grand courts with niched walls and many workshops for skilled artisans. Little of this complex survived after much of the city was stricken by great floods in about AD 600. The destruction was so devastating that the exact nature of such buildings is not easy to determine, though houses depicted on Moche pots provide certain clues.

Two types of construction are illustrated on this Moche pottery: the more imposing adobe structures are shown as being built on a platform or pyramid; these appear to be either the houses of important people or possibly religious buildings; in some cases what appear to be groups of mourners or worshippers are shown in front of them. Other painted pots depict a more modest type of dwelling of a kind that may commonly be seen today in the nearby countryside; such houses are illustrated as open walled, possibly an artistic convention to enable the viewer to see the person or scene depicted inside the house.

Previous to the much more recent discovery of the Sipan tombs, yielding dramatic evidence of Moche burial practices, excavations of Moche sites had produced massive quantities of fine painted pots, but no burials remotely comparable to those of Sipan. Only one grave of the first Moche phase was found at the base of the Pyramid of the Sun. A few burials of Moche II were excavated at the foot of the western side of the Pyramid of the Moon. The typical stirrup-spout bottles of this phase differed only in detail from those of phase I; further variations occur in phase III, when the spout is wide and short, as in the two previous phases, but the upper part has a pronounced flare. In phase IV, whose stirrup-spout samples are by far the most numerous, the spout becomes taller than in previous phases.

In all, prior to the latest discoveries, more than 350 Moche burials had been scientifically excavated; of these many were found at major settlements that also contained impressive Moche-style pyramids. In the simpler burials, the body was merely wrapped in a plain cotton shroud and placed face upwards in a shallow pit. In the more elaborate finds the body was either wrapped in many shrouds and twined cane matting, or placed in a boxlike cane coffin.

Whilst no manifestly royal tomb had thus far been found, since those from the major sites had been so completely looted long ago, the available burials were suggestive of a highly stratified society.

As we have seen, Moche civilization is now known to have spread far beyond the original Río Moche Valley sites, and other valleys from the Río Piura to the north to the Río Nepeña Valley at some distance to the south of Moche contained at least one or two major monuments which, if smaller in size, presented similar features to those of the Río Moche Valley itself, which continued to flourish until about AD 600, both as an urban complex and as an important centre of government.

Records in Clay

Since the Mochica, like all Andean peoples, had no writing, any attempt to reconstruct their history and their way of life is fraught with obvious problems. However, no other people of the world, with the possible exception of the ancient Greeks, recorded so many details of their culture on their pottery as the Mochica. Clearly, as we shall see, this legacy in clay is rich in symbols that are constantly repeated and which are intended to convey a specific meaning. Notwithstanding the depredations of the *huaqueros*, a copious store of Mochica pottery survives; mainly unearthed some time before the great Huaca Rajada discoveries, they have been described and illustrated in Elizabeth Benson's book on the Mochica, which does ample justice to their quality and significance. The pots were obviously made by superb craftsmen, who are themselves never illustrated on these vessels. Countless pots offer representations of chieftains, and thus offer a foretaste of Mochica culture, some aspects of which were later to be confirmed by the rich store of unlooted royal burials more recently found at Huaca Rajada. Others show warriors in battle, ritual processions, fishing, the hunting of deer, together with pictures of boats, houses, as well as geographical features such as marshes and deserts. But notwithstanding their striking realism, they clearly also had a sacred function. They are both realist and surrealist. A pot in the shape of a squash may have a neck that turns into a bird's head; beans at times have legs and faces and carry weapons. Several pots from the Pyramid of the Moon, together with a wall painting, show animated objects such as weapons and warriors' garments; but the large helmets often have small human legs, clubs have faces and kilted skirts sprout tiny human features.

While religion plays a major part in this ceramic iconography, it is not easy to interpret. The supreme deity of the Moche apparently dwelt in the mountains. As described by Benson, he is often shown sitting on a platform or throne, surrounded by lofty peaks. Neither human nor involved in human affairs, he thus appears as a kind of impassionate *deus otiosus* who, as in certain other cultures, having created the world, withdraws into a remoteness from the affairs of men.

More frequently depicted than this creator is a god with a Chavin-type feline mouth, snake's-head earrings and a jaguar head-dress; snakes also extend from his belt. This second deity is depicted as a vigorous figure, with arms and legs in constant motion. He may perhaps be seen as an active representative of the supreme mountain deity, a kind of god-the-son. He is always fanged. Though at times he seems to be a sea god, he is essentially the deity of the coastal people, protecting them from sea monsters; typical of these are a fish and a crab monster; the former is half human, with human arms and legs; he usually holds a knife. The deity is at times accompanied by a small, spotted animal who follows him like a pet and occasionally nips the crab monster.

Music apparently played a major part in Mochica ritual, particularly in funerary rites. The fanged deity himself is depicted playing pan-pipes; examples of these have been found, sometimes lying beside the dead as if ready to be played.

Figure 6 Moche Dancers Playing Pan-pipes

Sacrificial themes also abound. Some take place in the mountains, as offerings of human life to the creator god, usually involving two victims. The other major sacrificial theme involves not the creator but the fanged god and seems to take place in the sea. Again, two victims are involved; one body rides the crest of a breaking wave, which the fanged

Figure 7 Moche Ruler with Musicians

god watches from beyond the wave. While the supreme god appears to be indifferent to the fate of his victims, the fanged god observes them closely.

Other vessels also illustrate human sacrifice, sometimes in the form of naked warriors with ropes round their necks. Trophy heads depicted on pottery confirm sacrificial decapitation. In one death scene, the victim is tied to a stake and abandoned to vultures; in other scenes birds peck at the eyes and genitalia of bound victims.

Numerous animals appear in Moche art, in many cases associated with religious practices. To give only a few examples of the many animals represented: bats, often half human, appear with trophy heads

Figure 8 Moche Ritual Dancers

and are associated with human sacrifice and ritual. Hawks appear frequently; usually also anthropomorphic, these serve as warriors and messengers, as also do hummingbirds. Deer act as messengers and occasionally as warriors; deer with human arms sometimes are shown; in one scene the deer is sitting, holding two young deer as a human mother would. One group of effigy pots consists of birds and foxes, together with deer or seals seated and playing a drum.

Figure 9 Anthropomorphic Crab

Warfare is naturally a major theme in this rich documentation provided by Moche ceramics. One curious feature of such scenes is that while the chief deity is shown in combat with monsters, he never appears as a leader in human battles and pots in which this god carries conventional arms are very rare.

The warlike nature of the Moche is amply illustrated in their pottery and great numbers exist both of painted battle scenes and of effigy warriors. The latter wear knives attached to their belts, but these are never used in battle scenes. The main weapon is a large club and on the defensive arm is a square or round shield. At times the Moche fight

Figure 10 Moche Warrior with Prisoner

each other in hand-to-hand combat, and in other cases, to judge by the peculiar garb of the defeated warriors, these are depicted as foreigners. Such ceramic scenes suggest that they did not fight to kill but to take prisoners, since no one is ever shown dead in battle; some scenes illustrate naked prisoners seated, apparently awaiting ceremonial decapitation.

While in actual battle scenes the combatants who take prisoners are always human, in another category of painted pots figures in warriors' dress are shown; appearing usually in pairs, they have the faces of

Figure 11 Dismemberment of Captives

26

hummingbirds, hawks, owls, foxes, deer or even snakes. Another curious character is that of a warrior with the body of a lima bean.

Some painted pots show human figures running through a landscape, apparently carrying bags containing beans. Like the pots representing warriors, those representing runners sometimes show humans, and in others anthropomorphic animals of all kinds act as runners. In two cases animal-headed runners are shown as approaching a pyramid or temple; in one of these the deity sits on top of the temple, as if the runner seems to be his messenger or servant.

Figure 12 Moche Bird Warrior

Various aspects of the Moche economy are also shown on pots. Many depict rafts; often a deity is shown in the boat, but even if such scenes are partly mythological, such rafts were surely used by men who actually went to sea; shellfish are abundantly represented on the pottery. Numerous food plants cultivated by the Mochica are also illustrated, including maize, lima beans, peanuts, sweet potato, peppers, as well as various forms of squash. The importance of maize is indicated by representations, many of which show the head of the fanged deity emerging from the ears of maize. Lima beans also play a special role; they are the only vegetable that is truly anthropomorphic; with heads, arms and legs, lima beans are shown as warriors and messengers in both painted and modelled versions.

Finally, birth and death were also subjects that are often depicted on Moche ceramics. Before the great Sipan discoveries, one of the most important burials is that known as the tomb of the Warrior Priest at the Huaca de la Cruz in the Río Viru Valley. There are, however, many dead people illustrated on Moche pottery. Both in pots and modelled figures, the dead are usually shown with skulls and bony ribs. They are nude and the penis is often erect.

Another most curious feature is the appearance of the dead in scenes of sexual activity. Such depictions form part of a large corpus of erotic Mochica art; kissing is almost non-existent and an odd phenomenon is the frequent illustration of anal coitus. Fellatio, the contact between the female mouth and the male sex organ, was also a common theme.

Explanation both as to the abundance of Mochica erotic pottery and its peculiar features is hard to find. Rafael Larco-Hoyle found many erotic pots in graves of children, while in other graves skeletal figures perform sexual acts, but never coitus, and it becomes difficult to conclude that such pottery was mere pornography. On the other hand, if these scenes were viewed in a ceremonial or religious context, they would logically be connected with the notion of fertility, as the prominent sexual organs might suggest; but if that were the case, why do so many pots show anal coitus?

Huaca Rajada

Having first reviewed the data on Moche culture already obtained before the late 1980s, it now becomes appropriate to relate in more detail the story of the discoveries at Huaca Rajada, some 170 kilometres to the north of the Río Moche pyramids. In the words of Sidney Kirkpatrick, they represent a quantum leap in our knowledge, as compared with anything previously achieved.

As already stated, it was the looter Ernil Bernal who discovered the first royal burial chambers. After working at a feverish pace, he and his team-mates emerged haggard and exhausted, carrying eleven rice sacks filled with treasure – enough, in the words of one of the looters, to 'turn the poorest of them into the richest *hacienda* owner of the coastal plains'.

Other treasure hunters were not slow to enter the field and heated arguments then led to a shoot-out. However, it was not until two weeks later that the chief of the local police, Walter Mondragon, contacted Dr Walter Alva, inspector general of archaeology in Lambayeque, and director of the local Bruning Museum. Alva had, of course, known of the massive scale of looting of local sites, much of which had taken place in the past five years, but had been powerless to prevent this continuous process of plunder. At first, however, Alva thought that the report of the chief of police was little more than a hoax, since Huaca Rajada was not commonly associated with Moche but with the Chimu, a much later pre-Inca culture.

But together with the golden head of a puma, clearly a Moche work of art, Mondragon handed Alva fistfuls of shiny gold beads and, among other treasures, a ceremonial gold rattle in the shape of a half moon. To cite Kirkpatrick: 'Incised upon it was indisputable confirmation of the origin of the artefacts: the carved figure of a fearsome Moche deity holding a ceremonial knife in one hand and the decapitated head of a prisoner in the other. Alva was left speechless . . . the *huaqueros* had discovered something of which most archaeologists doubted the existence: the intact tomb of a Moche lord.'

From that point onwards, singular events followed in quick succession. First, before a caravan of eight policemen reached the Bernal house, Alva had already made the horrendous discovery in a nearby irrigation ditch of the smashed remains of some 250 ceramic vases, together with a large quantity of copper ornaments and some jewellery. Only the most saleable treasures had been retained, and already dispatched to antiquities dealers in Lima and Trujillo.

The fate of these treasures led to some bizarre consequences. Typical of these it may be worth citing a single incident. Among the first of the international dealers in stolen art to arrive on the scene was Don Poli. He first collected from his bank in Lima $40,000; the bank could only produce small denomination bills and he arrived in Trujillo with three suitcases containing his bundle of cash. Here he came into contact with a local dealer, who used the pseudonym Pereda. After protracted negotiations, Pereda produced a single piece (of the many of which he apparently disposed), a palm-sized statue of a Moche lord, its eyes encrusted with lapis lazuli. In one hand the lord had a finely carved shield and in his other hand a gold pyramid-shaped rattle. Poli settled for a price of $75,000 ($35,000 in excess of the contents of his suitcases of small bills). After a protracted search of the countryside, Poli finally returned with an entire carful of even smaller bills in cardboard boxes and shopping bags, in order to complete the payment of the $75,000.

Poli was eventually able to accumulate a major share of the original loot from Huaca Rajada. Unlike others involved, he escaped major litigation and imprisonment either in Peru or in the USA (to which many other pieces had been shipped). He also managed to have 170 pieces of looted Huaca Rajada treasure registered with the Peruvian National Institute of Culture as their legal owner! Some of Poli's comments to the police were included in an information agency's report to the President of the United States, a report which eventually, in June of 1991, led to a stricter enforcement of antiquities regulations and in particular a ban on the importation of all artefacts from Huaca Rajada.

Apart from Poli's haul, much royal treasure extracted by the looters did reach the USA by somewhat circuitous routes. Prominent among those involved was David Swetnam, a professional dealer in pre-Columbian objects. One of his methods for smuggling these works of art into the USA was to cover them with a cream-coloured clay slip, after which they could then be taken for contemporary pots made by Amazonian Shipibo Indians.

Many of Swetnam's customers were among the richest Californians, including Hollywood film producers and Los Angeles real-estate developers, whom he courted with poolside cocktails and even sumptuous banquets. His career as a dealer ended when, following denunciation by certain informants, in March 1988 sixty armed customs agents launched the biggest raid and achieved the largest seizure of pre-Columbian art in United States history. (Most of this came not from Huaca Rajada, but from yet another royal Moche burial chamber discovered at La Mina, located south of Lambayeque.) In all, 1369 artefacts were seized.

The ensuing litigation produced few results, since the judicial process was brought to a virtual standstill by a crack legal defence team, though Swetnam himself did receive a prison sentence of six months. In the end a mere 123 works of Peruvian art forfeited by United States collectors were returned to Peru. A ceremony was held on 2 December 1989 at Lima airport to celebrate this event, to which Enrique Poli, the proud and legal possessor of the largest privately held collection of Huaca Rajada gold, was not invited!

The Royal Tombs

The astonishing series of events outlined above relates more to the ultimate fate of the looted treasures and of the looters themselves and their wealthy clients.

Far more significant in the context of Moche studies was the decision of Alva on 13 April 1987 that he himself would undertake the excavation of the remainder of Huaca Rajada, after police had already cleared the site both of plunderers and of demonstrators who protested against hitherto ineffective police action.

Even more decisive was the arrival four days later of the most distinguished Moche scholar, Christopher Donnan. Alva was familiar with Donnan's two books on the Moche; hence his reputation preceded him when he arrived at the Bruning Museum and introduced himself to Alva. The story of what followed is described by Donnan in the fine catalogue of the exhibition held in the Fowler Museum of Los Angeles, the New York Natural History Museum and other prestigious institutions, which displayed the magnificent Huaca Rajada discoveries.

Donnan's account stresses that the ruins near Sipan had been virtually unknown before the recent work began. The two large truncated pyramids were connected by a complex series of ramps; the third and smaller pyramid, where the tomb had been looted, appears to have been free-standing, connected to the larger pyramids only by a plaza.

This huge complex had been constructed over a period of many years and had undergone many changes. It was clearly a Moche creation, though certain evidence suggests that further changes occurred after the end of the Moche era. The small pyramid, as we have seen, had been the object of a much more aggressive attack on the part of the looters. Paradoxically, the looters' backdirt had helped to preserve the structure's original form and subtle features of its architecture showed that it had also been the product of successive periods of construction.

In its earliest phase it appears to have been merely a low, rectangular platform; Donnan suggests that this phase may belong to the first century AD, and was followed by five further stages of which the last was completed in AD 300.

Most surprisingly, the looters had missed some of the original objects in the tomb which they penetrated. Of these, by far the most remarkable was a heavy copper sceptre, one metre long, with a point at one end and a complex architectural model at the other, consisting of a small structure with a gabled roof. On the ridgeline of the roof were seventeen double-faced human heads. The back portion, formed by a wall, depicted a haunting scene: a supernatural creature, half feline and half reptile, copulating with a woman riding on a crescent moon. This sceptre surely formed part of the ceremonial paraphernalia of a very high-status Moche lord.

Alva and Donnan recognized this creature as the supreme Moche spirit in its most fearsome incarnation, half feline and half reptile. Mouth open and claws extended, the fanged deity plunged its penis deep between the female victim's spread legs.

Tomb 1

Alva and Donnan decided not to initiate a large dig at the summit of the main complex, which would be too vulnerable to looters once the excavation ended.

A preliminary study of a ten-by-ten-metre area a little below the summit yielded a remarkable collection of fine ceramics; a total of 1137 vessels were removed from a chamber that held probably the largest offering of pre-Columbian ceramics ever discovered.

As this chamber was studied, another area slightly to the south-east was examined. First a single skeleton of a man was discovered about four metres below the original surface of the pyramid. But some fifty centimetres beneath this burial were found the remains of large wooden beams. One fact was evident: the pattern of these roof beams was intact and whatever chamber lay below had remained for ever undisturbed. In penetrating the chamber they first found an adult male aged between 35 and 50 years at the time of his death. The left foot was missing. His body was covered with copper objects and alongside lay a large war-club, encased in copper sheet. On the other side of the royal burial itself was another cane coffin placed on top of a sacrificed llama; it contained a male victim between 35 and 45 years old.

The wood of the coffin of the royal burial itself had long since decomposed. However, its contents were still intact and as described by Walter Alva and Christopher Donnan constituted the richest burial ever excavated anywhere in the western hemisphere, and would there-fore prove to be one of the most significant archaeological discoveries of our generation. To name only a few of the objects found: on top of the royal head-dress was a large gold ingot; the metal was so pure that its surface remained uncorroded.

Much of the area inside the coffin was covered over with beaded pectorals. Such pectorals had never been excavated archaeologically; the task proved a formidable challenge, and their removal took several weeks.

As they thus came closer to the body itself, the quantity and quality of the personal ornaments dramatically increased. To cite only a single example of the copious treasures: the most amazing of the ear ornaments was a pair depicting warriors. Meticulously detailed, the two warriors stood about the size of a man's thumb, each holding a war-club in his clenched fist. The figures wore no fewer than four necklaces, including one consisting of sixteen gold links depicting human heads. The deceased clenched in his right hand a large gold and silver sceptre; the sceptre held in his left hand had an elaborate finial at its upper end.

Three other cane coffins contained adult females, two of which were stacked one on top of the other at the head of the main tomb, while the third lay at its foot. On examination, a strange fact emerged: these female skeletal remains suggest that they had died long before the principal figure and that their bodies were partially decomposed when they were placed in his tomb. The bones were jumbled in ways that could not have occurred through an *in situ* decomposition of their bodies. There is no evidence as to how long the women had been dead; it is even possible that they may have been dead before the principal male was even born!

When all these additional coffins had already been put in place, the whole tomb had then been sealed by the beam roof. Since it was only slightly higher than the benches that extended along the sides of the chamber, the roof was too low to have created a room in which people entering later could have stood upright.

Tomb 2

While work on this tomb was still in progress, other parts of the pyramid were also examined. At one point, 2.4 metres below ground surface, a llama skull was found; a few centimetres lower was an adult male lying on his back, buried in a cane coffin. Like the burial situated above Tomb 1, the man's feet were missing. After removing the roof beams a plank coffin was found, smaller than that of Tomb 1, but none the less indicative that this was also a royal burial.

In addition to many fine ornaments, the occupant of this tomb wore two extraordinary necklaces of human-head beads; the faces were smiling on one necklace and frowning on the other. The motif of complementary smiling and frowning faces was heretofore unknown in ancient Peruvian art and remains an unexplained mystery.

The individual in question was an adult male, some forty years old, and 1.5 metres tall. Unlike the first tomb, this principal figure himself wore no lavish jewellery and ornaments. However, beneath where his head rested was found a spectacular head-dress ornament of gilded copper; at its centre were the head and body of an owl, whose eyes were inlaid with white shell and turquoise. On each side of the principal figure lay the remains of a young female with no coffin, while crosswise to his feet was the body of a ten-year-old child placed in a coffin that also contained the skeletons of a dog and a snake.

The main difference between the two tombs was one of scale. Not only was Tomb 2 smaller, but there were considerably fewer grave contents, and with certain exceptions, of lower quality.

As these offerings on the south platform were excavated, yet a third royal tomb was found, lying more than five metres below the surface of the pyramid. It soon became evident that since it was below the later burials, the tomb was earlier than those described above. The principal body was placed not in a room-sized chamber, but in a simple pit; it had no plank coffin but was wrapped in several textile shrouds.

None the less, this earlier tomb yielded many fine works of art, including a magnificent gold necklace of ten large beads, and depicting a spider with a body in the form of a human head. Another masterpiece was a feline head made of gilded copper; the ferocious expression of its face was enhanced by a double-headed serpent head-dress. Both around and above the body lay multiple sets of the finest necklaces, ear ornaments, and nose ornaments of gold and silver piled one on top of another in a dazzling display of wealth and opulence, too numerous to describe in detail. Finally the excavators reached the actual body; the skull was fairly well preserved, and the skeletal remains were of an adult aged about fifty, 1.6 metres tall. A large gold ingot had been placed in his mouth and two large silver ingots were placed on top of his chin.

The Moche Realm

Certainly one of the major lessons to be learned from the Sipan tombs is that the Moche culture was even more refined and complex than we had previously realized, notwithstanding the copious data already supplied by activities depicted on Moche ceramics, above all available in the photographic archive located on the campus of the University of California at Los Angeles.

But no burials previously excavated bore even a remote comparison with those of Sipan, nor had they yielded objects of a comparable refinement.

From illustrations of such earlier finds the essence of Moche warfare was shown to be not mass battles, but rather the exercise of individual valour in which warriors engaged in single combat. Great stress is placed on the capture of prisoners, who were taken to a place where they could be arraigned before a high individual in the vicinity of a large pyramid. Following arraignment, the prisoners were ceremoniously sacrificed by the cutting of their throats, and their blood was ritually consumed by those present. In a typical scene, the leading figure is designated as the Warrior Priest, accompanied by the Bird Priest and the Bird Priestess.

A most significant feature of Tomb 1 is that nearly all the objects found in that tomb were related to the sacrifice ceremony as already

Figure 13 Consumption of Ritual Blood by Priest

depicted on ceramics unearthed in previous decades. To cite a single example: the duck is often illustrated in the latter as an anthropomorphized warrior who participates in the sacrifice ceremony. The duck also appears on gold and turquoise ear ornaments in Tomb 1, which may be related to his involvement in the ceremony where prisoners were ritually slain.

The Warrior Priest mentioned above was consistently represented with a large conical helmet with crescent-shaped ornaments, large circular ear ornaments, bracelets, and a warrior back-flap. He frequently wears a crescent-shaped nose ornament. Each of these items was also found inside the plank coffin of the central figure of Tomb 1.

The relative longevity of the Moche civilization has already been stressed and recent research has added a new perspective to our knowledge of its refinement, complexity, and even of its extent. Sipan is situated some 150 kilometres to the north of the great pyramids of the Río Moche Valley; moreover, from what we have now learned from the intact burial chambers of Sipan, it now becomes almost certain that the massive quantities of fine metal objects, looted by robbers in the 1960s from the site of Loma Negra, situated yet a further 200 kilometres to the north of Sipan, also were taken from tombs of high-status Moche princes.

Moreover, at a congress held in Trujillo in 1993, while not rejecting Larco-Hoyle's original five phases of Moche culture, it was stressed that elements recalling Moche I and Moche II were also found in these northerly settlements. Hence Moche sites, both early and late, are known to have occupied a very long stretch of the Pacific coast.

Less is known of Moche political organization and it becomes most questionable whether anything in the nature of an overall Moche kingdom existed rather than a series of settlements that shared a common culture.

The central figure of the complex tombs of Sipan is more generally described as a Warrior Priest. None the less, in view of the distances involved between many Moche sites, it might be logical to assume that such individuals, buried with so much elaborate ceremony, were in practice more likely to have been independent potentates rather than subjects or representatives of some kind of Moche 'emperor' situated in the Río Moche Valley or elsewhere. Their situation was perhaps more comparable to that of the independent principalities of Renaissance Italy than to the unified kingdoms of England or France.

CHAPTER THREE

NAZCA: UNSOLVED ENIGMAS

An Astounding Discovery

To the south of Lima the Peruvian coastline becomes even more austere. The desert landscape is relieved only by a few river valleys, which present a lush contrast to the endless sand dunes. About 400 kilometres south of Lima lies an elevated plateau, situated 75 kilometres inland at an altitude of 500 metres, bounded on the north by the Río Ingenio and on the south and west by the Río Nazca.

In contrast to the two river valleys, this stark stretch of brown pebbles, devoid of plant or animal life, is known as the Nazca Pampa.

However, when first surveyed from an aircraft in 1926, this bleak expanse astounded its viewers; the pampa was seen to be carpeted with man-made designs. These included highly realistic outlines of animals and plants; interspersed between these more imaginative shapes, a plethora of straight lines were seen to fan out in all directions; some of these ran for many miles. This discovery presented archaeologists with a formidable challenge since none could offer any conceivable explanation as to why at some time in antiquity a stretch of bare desert had been thus elaborately adorned.

The Nazca lines, henceforth treated as a new wonder of the American Ancient World, have featured in countless magazines, in worldwide television shows, and in many books, including works on the occult. They became the source of endless speculation; some favoured the notion that the Nazcans somehow soared over the pampa in a prehistoric form of glider or in hot-air balloons, since from ground level they could not have observed their work as we are able to do today. Among other theorists, Erich von Däniken, the intrepid champion of extraterrestrial visits to Earth, entered the field; in his book, *Chariots of the Gods*, the lines are described as runways for craft from outer space, a notion already put forth by George Hunt Williamson in his book, *Road in the Sky*, which contained a chapter on Nazca entitled 'Beacons for the Gods'.

Von Däniken, who acquired an immense following, intrigued by his insistence on the extraterrestrial origins of human civilization, tends to seek, like Faust, one answer to every question. For this author every shaven head on a statue is really a spaceman's helmet, every outstretched hand is described as clutching a spaceship's lever, and every stylized moth becomes an aircraft! Not content with the notion that the Prophet Ezekiel saw and described a spacecraft, he even proclaimed that certain birds and insects in the Gold Museum of Bogotá are really extraterrestrial aircraft. Perhaps, therefore, it is hardly surprising that in *Chariots of the Gods* the author reproduced a photo from Nazca that he describes as depicting 'parking bays', resembling those of a modern airport. But he failed to perceive that such markings in fact represented the right knee and four claws that form one part of the outline of a giant bird.

When directly challenged and confronted with a complete drawing of this bird in a BBC television film, also shown in the United States, he for once admitted that he had erred and that his picture of 'parking bays' was a mistake. But he merely modified his stance and in another book, *Return to the Stars*, he again claimed that space visitors had used Nazca as an improvised airport.

In fairness to von Däniken it must be stated that other writers have also indulged in such far-fetched notions. For instance, Jim Woodman, to prove the existence of prehistoric balloons, in his book *Nazca. Journey to the Sun*, tells how he himself piloted a crude hot-air balloon over the pampa in 1975. The balloon was constructed from materials found in ancient times in shrouds taken from Nazca graves.

In 1983 a Swiss author, Henri Stierlin, produced an even odder theory, insisting that the Nazca lines were somehow connected with textile workshops and hence with the making of the huge burial shrouds that formed part of the Nazca culture.

In seeking more plausible solutions, one is first struck by the bleakness of the setting. In contrast to the lush valley of the Río Nazca lying to the south, the pampa on which the lines are drawn is almost totally arid; over a nine-year period between 1957 and 1965, the average precipitation was measured as 4.53 millimetres per annum; in six of these nine years annual rainfall was less than 2 millimetres. No studies have been made of the climate that might have prevailed in earlier times when the first lines were presumably created, but data from other parts of the coast of southern Peru suggest that there have been no major changes in the last few thousand years.

Viewed from the air, the Nazca lines present a confused picture, intersecting each other in such a way as to give an impression not unlike the remains of an unerased blackboard at the end of a busy day of classroom activities. The pampa surface reveals details of countless figures that overlap each other; clearly, therefore, a great deal of human effort must have been devoted to their creation, probably stretching over a fairly long period of time.

The forms represented consist on the one hand of straight lines, rectangles, spirals and trapezoids; but apart from the straight lines and spirals, other designs illustrate plants and animals, including fish, birds, a monkey and a spider as well as other creatures that are harder to identify. Most animals are on a fairly small scale, as compared with the immense length and complexity of some lines; only a few of the animals are large, such as a huge spider and a bird whose outline extends for 300 metres. In general straight lines dominate; apart from these lines and zigzags there are also more than a hundred spiral forms, some of which are of an extraordinary complexity. A few most unusual designs have been noted, including a peculiar five-armed paddle wheel.

While the animal figures are localized in one area, they are significant as a mode of artistic expression. Forms such as those of a killer whale, a lizard and a frigate bird are very similar to those found on Nazca ceramics.

Nazca: Its People and Their Art

Much has been written on the Nazca lines and on the purposes which they might have served. But it becomes hard to consider such questions unless one first studies the culture and antecedents of the people who presumably created them. As Anthony Aveni observes in his major

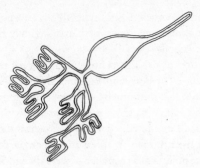

Figure 14 Nazca Lines: Plant

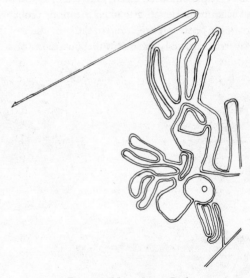

Figure 15 Nazca Lines: Bird

work on Nazca, *Order in the Nazca Lines?*, too little discussion of Nazca origins, and hence of the earlier cultures on the south coast of Peru, appears in the literature about the lines, concerning which basic questions require to be asked in a pan-Andean framework.

It is important to note that comparatively early studies, such as those of the Columbia University expedition of 1952, described Nazca culture as springing from the much earlier style of Paracas, a peninsula situated some 160 kilometres north-west of Nazca, with which it shares a comparable climate.

Shortly after the turn of this century, magnificent textiles began to appear in collections in Peru and Europe. Well-preserved and richly embroidered, they attracted much attention, though their provenance was unclear. The source of these garments was first identified in the late 1920s, when Julio Tello visited the Paracas peninsula. Similar textiles were excavated from burials in three zones named Cavernas, Arena Blanca and Necropolis. These cemeteries were the work of people who are now known to have lived in Paracas from approximately 600 to 175 BC. The principal burials, those of the Necropolis, cover a span of almost 300 years, from 475 to 175 BC. Decorated bowls and bottles from Paracas bear a distinct relationship to the final phase of the Chavin culture, Janabarriu, probably dating from about 400 to 200 BC.

Figure 16 Paracas Painted Vessels

The people of Paracas were most versatile, and produced not only pottery but finely worked stone clubs, obsidian knives, shell and bone necklaces, together with hammered gold ornaments and fine feather fans.

Anne Paul, a leading authority on Paracas, describes the people's leaders as dressed in magnificent woven apparel, embellished with images embroidered in vivid colours. These fine outer garments concealed decorated tunics, ponchos and skirts. When each chief died, he was carefully wrapped with precious garments worn in life and with other textiles offered as gifts. The burial bundles were interred in the large Necropolis cemetery; such bundles form the main record of Paracas culture.

The Necropolis contained 429 bundles. Under Julio Tello's supervision over forty of the largest were unwrapped and are housed in the National Museum of Anthropology and Archaeology in Lima. Moved from one depository to another, flooded by rain water, eaten by insects, and ravaged by the damp Lima climate, many have suffered more damage in the past sixty years than in the previous two thousand. Incidentally, six of the largest bundles were loaned to the Ibero-American Exposition in Seville in 1929 and never returned!

None the less, enough of these splendid remains have survived to enable Anne Paul to write a most explicit book, published in 1990, on Paracas ritual attire, replete with fine illustrations; the text describes certain Paracas textiles as deriving from the earliest motifs of the Nazca–Ica region.

The Nazca culture may be viewed in many respects as the direct successor of Paracas, since it flourished from about 200 BC to AD 600. In Nazca, pottery rather than weaving became the paramount art form; Nazca embroidery was simpler and less refined. The painted images, however, clearly display many of the themes that figured in the Paracas textiles.

The Gothenburg Ethnographic Museum of Sweden has a unique collection of pots that illustrate the typical themes of the Nazca style. A frequent and strange image portrays a man standing frontally, out of whose mouth emerges a serpent tongue that ends in one or sometimes two trophy heads. The man has an elaborate head-dress, consisting either of weird animals or of another human face. Other Nazca pots display features more directly derived from Paracas, such as a figure bearing a winged forehead badge with a trailing appendage, accompanied by severed human heads, a dominant Paracas theme. At times a more docile striped catlike creature appears, that often clutches fruit or vegetables, obviously symbols of fertility; some early Nazca pots portray unique images of beans or peppers.

Figure 17 Images on Nazca Painted Pots

A peculiar feature of this Nazca culture, whose potters developed such refined skills, is that it was based on no major centres of population comparable, say, to those of the Moche, let alone the monumental site of later date at Chan Chan. It seems that Nazca pots were produced in a number of smaller settlements spread over a fairly wide area; notwithstanding certain local variations, the basic themes were simply repeated from one valley to the next. We find no large and complex ruins in the area, suggestive of the existence of some kind of Nazca 'empire', and no traces exist of storage facilities and administrative buildings more typical of a conquest state. Instead, the evidence suggests that the Nazca peoples were simply scattered across a series of semi-fertile valleys.

Cahuachi

As a partial exception to this demographic pattern, the fairly large site of Cahuachi, lying to the west of the settlement of Nazca itself, may be cited. It had previously been suggested that Cahuachi was an aggress-ive and even militaristic centre, based on the numerous pots displaying severed heads, together with actual human heads dug up within the site. More recently intensive fieldwork has been carried out by Helaine

Silverman, described in a massive book on Cahuachi published in 1993. While the author stresses that Cahuachi, which flourished from about AD 1 to 750, is by far the largest known site of the Nazca culture, she lends no support to notions of the site as a strictly urban centre. In 85 per cent of its total area there is no evidence of residential occupation; the remaining 15 per cent consists of lightly modified hills which constitute Cahuachi's only form of monumental construction. The forty semi-artificial mounds of varying size and form seem to serve ceremonial rather than domestic purposes. Only a single intact temple precinct was discovered on one small mound. As a group of scattered sacred points on a profane landscape, Cahuachi itself became sacred more by the nature of the rites performed than by the presence of impressive monuments.

Silverman, moreover, does not see the site as having attained the commercial significance of certain other pilgrimage centres, in particular Pachacamac. There are few storage facilities and material goods brought thither were rapidly consumed. Hence Cahuachi conveys the impression of a ceremonial centre that could either be bustling with activity or virtually depopulated, depending on the day.

The same author suggests that such activities might imply the ritual consumption of fair amounts of Nazca pottery. The role of Cahuachi is perhaps less to be compared to that of Pachacamac than to the modern pilgrimage shrine at Yauca in the Ica Valley, some 190 kilometres to the north, known as the Sanctuary of the Virgin of the Rosary of Yauca. It is used occasionally rather than continuously and it would appear that Cahuachi, like Yauca, lacked a residential population of any size. For the Festival of the Virgin, thousands of peasants remain camped outside the plaza area of Yauca, itself transformed into a great market with close-packed kiosks. A few days later the site may be abandoned and the 'city' dismembered almost as quickly as it was installed.

Of notable significance was the discovery by Silverman of many trophy heads, so abundantly illustrated in early Nazca pottery. One such head wore an elaborately braided coiffure; in another, a carrying cord emerges from a hole in the frontal bone. On the basis of mortuary remains collected in Cahuachi and other places, she suggests that approximately 5 per cent of the whole Nazca population ended up as trophy heads or headless bodies!

Scores of smaller domestic sites contemporary with Cahuachi have been discovered, most of which are under four hectares in size. Only one, Ventilla, is larger and covers 200 hectares. Hence, in considering the sociopolitical context of the famous Nazca style, early notions of Cahuachi as the capital of a centralized state, let alone a militaristic empire, become even harder to accept. In Nazca pottery no social hierarchy is clearly illustrated, as for example in Moche art. Cahuachi and other early Nazca sites are to be seen more as a kind of interacting group of separate societies linked by a shared religious tradition. The possibility is not totally to be excluded of some kind of formal chiefdom in which paramountcy might have rotated, but with Cahuachi as its seat. However, the absence of residential or administrative constructions at that site would make the existence of even such a broad-based chiefdom seem highly questionable.

No Simple Answers

In the early 1930s many flights were made over the Nazca Pampa and the notion thus tended to prevail that the lines could only be appreciated and understood when thus seen from above. Such flights attracted much attention, but apart from a brief study by Mejia Xesspe, a well-known Peruvian archaeologist, published in 1939, the first person to seek more concrete conclusions was Paul Kosok, a New Yorker with wide-ranging interests. (At one time he had been a conductor of the Brooklyn Civic Orchestra.)

Kosok's first visit to Nazca took place in 1941, and in his brief season of research he studied a series of lines and several large rectangular shapes together with a strange, stylized image of a bird. He became convinced at this early stage that the lines had some astronomical significance. Kosok did not return to Nazca until 1948. He then worked there for some time, though his principal book, *Life, Land and Water in Ancient Peru*, did not appear until 1965.

His research was continued by María Reiche, a German mathematics teacher who had already worked with Julio Tello at the Paracas site. Reiche agreed to take over the detailed study of Kosok's drawings, and during the following period spent as many hours each year in Nazca as she could afford; for the remainder of her time she worked in a tea shop in Lima. She used to stay in an old hotel in the town of Nazca, getting up at 3 a.m. to hitch a ride from trucks that passed along the Panamerican Highway. This remarkable woman devoted her whole life to the enigma of Nazca. Apart from a much publicized television film, *Mystery on the Desert*, she wrote several books and many articles on the subject. In the earlier years of her long sojourn she was largely ignored by the local people, who assumed that she was a kind of mad witch. They themselves at this stage had little awareness of the desert markings because they are so difficult to view from the ground.

Standing on a two-metre ladder, Reiche could recognize not only spirals and trapezoids; she also identified animal figures, such as the killer whale and a giant bird that resembled a condor. But she was even more struck by a figure recognizable as a monkey that measured eighty metres from head to tail. Since such animals were unknown in the Nazca Valley and do not appear on its painted pots, this posed a further puzzle. Convinced that the figure must also be of astronomical significance, she claimed that at the time when the lines were drawn the form of a monkey could have been seen in the sky, made up from various stars, including the Great Bear. On checking the compass angles of the straight lines near the monkey drawing, she found a long track that pointed to the star Benetnasch, as it would have risen above the horizon in about the year AD 1000. This star is at the tip of the tail, or handle, of the Great Bear constellation.

Though for many years Reiche was thus left to pursue her studies in comparative tranquillity, all this was to change as Nazca came to be the object of a massive burst of publicity; particularly after the publication in 1968 of von Däniken's book, depicting Nazca as a landing ground for spaceships, the pampa was invaded overnight with cars, motor cycles and even trekkers with donkeys!

Both Kosok and Reiche had become obsessed with the notion that the main significance of the lines was astronomical. Kosok based this contention on a study of social developments which he associated with early Nazca times. He argued that any group that developed an elaborate agricultural system would require some understanding of astronomy, since the annual progress of the seasons was related to the movements of the stars, a process the precise nature of which could only be fathomed by a class of astronomer–priests; hence the lines were seemingly connected with methods of determining the relevant calendar dates.

Writing in more detail on the same theme, Reiche, to quote one example, cited the azimuth range of 68° 15' to 70° 10', stating that the Pleiades and Scorpio rose in this direction in AD 500–700 at the latitude of Nazca. Within this interval of 68° to 70°, Reiche backed her conclusions by citing various of her line measurements, including one side of a triangle, four scattered lines and sixteen zigzag segments of one single feature.

Though, as we shall see, astronomical solutions to the Nazca puzzle have since tended to be questioned, they still retain a certain influence. Scholars who have written more recently on the subject, such as Johann Reinhard, concur with other specialists that at least a few of the lines might have played a role in making astronomical observations. Reinhard himself, while admitting that the lines pose a problem for which there can be no single solution, was attracted above all by the notion that the triangles and trapezoid lines were somehow intended to draw down moisture from the foothills of the Andes to the east of Nazca.

Nazca and Stonehenge

Following the work of Kosok and of Reiche, whose principal work, *Mystery on the Desert*, was first published in 1948, many questions remained unanswered, notwithstanding her firm adherence to astronomical explanations.

It was not until 1968 that the astronomer Gerald Hawkins entered the field. In 1963 Hawkins had caused a sensation in the academic world when he published a paper, 'Stonehenge Decoded', in the British journal *Nature*. To test his theory, he drew lines between pairs of stones, pits and posts, which were then fed into a computer. At first many scientists questioned his conclusion that the layout of the famous site, built some 5000 years ago on Salisbury Plain, might be connected with stellar observations. However, his theory did come to achieve a measure of scientific acceptance and today few scholars doubt that the builders of Stonehenge were aware of the major cycles of the sun and moon.

Hawkins adopted the same approach to the problem of Nazca. With the help of cartographers at the Peruvian Geophysical Institute he first plotted a highly accurate map based on air photos. After having measured the directions of all the lines, he ran a similar computer program to that of Stonehenge, comparing the many different alignments with the movements of the sun, moon and stars along the horizon.

But of all the 186 possible alignments which Hawkins selected, only a very limited number correspond with the angles of the sun and moon to within a margin of one degree on either side. The remainder ran to all points of the compass, though a few pointed to a very mixed bag of heavenly bodies, including certain rather faint stars.

But since Hawkins was convinced that the astronomical theory could only be accepted if the lines pointed to a clear pattern of celestial events, he concluded that the methods applied to Stonehenge were invalid in the case of Nazca. Further computer tests affirmed this view, and the astronomical theory was pronounced by Hawkins as dead. Following his investigations the general opinion has prevailed among specialists that only a few Nazca lines might have played a role in making astronomical observations.

New Approaches

Since Hawkins's outright rejection of the lifelong conviction of Kosok and María Reiche that the Nazca lines were basically astronomical, countless scholars have entered the field, though none has so far offered any single explanation that is wholly convincing. Each tends to emphasize some particular aspect of the problem, without attempting to devise a more definitive overall solution.

Among such writers one may cite Tony Morrison, a British filmmaker who wrote much on the subject in the 1970s, including a book, *Pathways to the Gods*, that attracted considerable attention. He was much influenced by the work of the French anthropologist Alfred Métraux, who as early as 1934 had described pathways, made by the Chipaya Indians of Bolivia, who built many small shrines scattered in long rows at distances of up to ten miles from a village. What impressed Métraux most of all were straight lines or pathways cut through the vegetation, that converged on such isolated shrines like spokes on a wheel. Morrison led an expedition to Bolivia, where he was surprised to see lines running for over thirty kilometres near the slopes of Sajama, one of the highest mountains of Bolivia. He eventually reached the village of Sajama, lying at a height of 4250 metres. Here too he found straight paths leading in every direction, usually running up from churches to small villages. While these lines were quite different in construction to those of Nazca, Morrison's work served to draw attention to the possible ceremonial, as opposed to astronomical, functions of the Nazca lines.

Working in the 1980s, the anthropologist Johann Reinhard further explored the possible use of the Nazca lines for ceremonial purposes; working in the even more remote deserts of northern Chile, he discovered a strange cluster of drawings on a hill known as Cerro Unitas that recalled those of Nazca. A series of straight lines run up the *cerro*, each of which ends in a cairn near the summit. He thus clearly established an example of lines that served as sacred pathways to the shrines of Andean deities, a phenomenon that he linked with the need for water in arid regions.

However, in recent times the most comprehensive work on the Nazca lines is surely that of Anthony Aveni, who edited *Order in the Nazca Lines?*, published in 1990, describing his own work and also containing articles by other distinguished scholars.

As Aveni remarks, on reviewing the relevant literature, he was surprised to learn that only a handful of investigators had ever ventured into the desolate surface of the pampa to look at the lines close-up. He questions whether people had become too rigidly accustomed to view it from the air, the method by which the lines were discovered by those who flew over them in the 1920s, and asks whether the notion that they were meant to be seen from above had become an established dogma. Aveni further draws attention to the fact that a close study of the archaeological remains on the surface of the pampa (as opposed to lines seen mainly from the air) is vital to any understanding of why the lines were made. In reviewing past studies, he realized that no one had ever undertaken a thorough examination of the surface on which the lines and figures were drawn.

An exception to Aveni's observation on this point is the work of Persis Clarkson, of whom an article is included in Aveni's book. Gerald Hawkins had gathered some pottery fragments from three strips of the pampa surface; most of the shards that he collected dated from the relatively early periods, known as Nazca 3 and 4 (approximately 100 BC to AD 100). But such evidence used as a method of dating the lines conflicts notably with Clarkson's ground-level investigation of a different and much more extensive area of lines; she found very few shards associated with this early period and their presence cannot logically be taken as sure evidence that the makers of this pottery constructed the lines. Clarkson further points out that the surface geoglyphs illustrating birds and other animals are not necessarily contemporary with the finest Nazca ceramics, even if these glyphs illustrate birds and lizards of a kind that figure in this pottery.

Somewhat surprisingly, in the vicinity of many geoglyphs more pottery was found dating from a much later era, known as the Middle Horizon or Huari period, running from about AD 600 to 1000; however, as Clarkson observes, if these geoglyphs were really made during the Huari period, they bear little relationship to the very different concepts and motifs that then prevailed.

Aveni's account of his investigations first presents a copious review of every kind of previous study of the Nazca lines, some of which have been described above. He pays due tribute to the tireless work of María Reiche and describes some of her discoveries as tantalizing, if inexplicable. For instance, she discovered that in measuring trapezoids, lengths of 32.6 metres and its double occur frequently, as also do several doubles of 26.7 metres, a measurement that is cited in ten instances. Aveni even goes to great lengths to examine certain of Reiche's involved calculations, such as her analysis of the abdomen of a spider figure formed by a dozen segments that can somehow be tied to the cycle of lunar phases. He felt compelled, however, to conclude that such an analysis is quite arbitrary and is linked to no information about the culture that produced it. He concludes by stating that considerations of precise geometry contained within the Nazca lines are indeed tantalizing but inconclusive. He even includes an appendix on the Cantalloc spiral design that forms part of a much larger figure, but the results of his study proved basically negative, though he admits that the analysis of a single spiral should not close the door to further discussion. In another context, he states that stellar alignments and astronomy, though now largely discounted, may nevertheless be faintly present.

One of Aveni's main themes is an insistence that the lines were made to be walked upon. He mentions in this context an ingenious but not well-known study by the archaeologist H. Horkheimer, published in 1947. This Peruvian investigator considered that the trapezoids were intended as places of assembly for sacred reunions of cults of the dead, while the sacred dances that were performed might also be related to worship of the dead.

Aveni further cites, among the more imaginative explanations, the theory of G. von Breunig, expressed in his 1980 publication, *Nazca: A Pre-Columbian Olympic Site?* As this title implies, the author proposed that the lines might have been constructed for the purpose of running competitive races. While this idea may appear odd at first glance, plenty of evidence does exist that ritual walking, running or dancing were important in ancient Peru. For von Breunig, however, the running theory surely enters the realm of fantasy when he proposes that the lines first served for local races that culminated in a form of national games with athletically garbed participants, all supposedly to be found on Nazca pottery.

Before reviewing Aveni's comments on the vast network of straight lines, it may be useful first to consider the rather inexplicable geometrical figures formed by certain lines. Aveni's survey revealed a total of 227 such figures that cover a greater area of the pampa than the straight lines, together with the animal and plant designs. Such geometrical figures are triangles and rectangles, though the term 'trapezoid' usually serves to designate them all. The figures are very large and twenty-four of them cover areas larger than 45,000 square metres! Four-sided square trapezoids comprise 62 per cent of all geometrical figures examined, while triangles form 27 per cent of the total; rectangles make up only 9 per cent of the sample. The purpose of such forms is hard to explain, but the suggestion is made that the builders may have intended to establish some sense of local orientation with respect to water flow, a subject that will be treated in more detail below.

The purpose of the animal and plant figures may be even harder to explain. Some three dozen examples of these biomorphic Nazca figures are almost all located in a relatively small area of the pampa. They also may have been intended to be walked upon, rather than viewed from on high. While it has been suggested that the animal and geometrical figures are related, Aveni inclines to the view that they may represent activities undertaken by entirely different groups of people at different times. In this respect it may be worth noting that, though many of the animal species etched on the pampa can also be found on typical Nazca ceramics, dating from about 200 BC to AD 600, as we have seen above, the shards found near these zooglyphs mostly belong to a later period.

A Major Conclusion

By walking upon the pampa and taking careful measurements, Aveni reached a new conclusion of major significance. As he observes, while so much attention had been devoted to the animal and plant figures, the width and length of the vast network of lines had scarcely been tabulated by modern investigators, although far more manpower and planning had been devoted in ancient times to these straight features. Many photographs indicated clearly that interconnecting patterns of lines could be identified. Moreover, certain of Reiche's maps contained lines that seemed to converge on what she had called 'star-like centers', or 'networks'.

Using an enlargement of one of these maps, and removing from the enlargement all features other than the straight lines, Aveni and Garry Urton studied a fifty-square-kilometre strip of the desert bordering the south bank of the Río Ingenio Valley (which constitutes the northern extremity of the area marked by lines), and were able to identify four specific points from which a total of eighty-eight lines emanated or converged in a spoke pattern; not a single line could be found that did not connect to one of these focal points. Subsequently they walked over some lines in the same area that were directed towards other star-like focal centres on the other side of the pampa.

Previous studies of the lines from ground-based research had been rare, and offered little detailed information. In contrast, Aveni and Urton spent long periods of time walking the lines, in many cases as far as their termination point. Having studied the four spoked patterns already explored, they examined the area to the south, bordering on the Río Nazca Valley, and discovered a further five focal-line centres. They soon realized that these line centres had certain common features:

they all consisted of a group of natural hills or mounds, and most are located in that part of the pampa where the last hill can be seen to descend from the higher mountains. These hills were nearly all situated along the elevated rim of the pampa that borders the principal rivers and their tributaries; few line centres were found in the middle of the pampa. In all, 762 lines were tabulated, emanating from 62 focal centres. Of these, 224 lines were classified as broad and 538 as narrow. The average traceable length of a line from its centre is 13 kilometres. The longest is over 19 kilometres. Only one single line was found that was not demonstrably tied to one of the 62 centres.

While no one has challenged the demonstrable layout of the lines in this spoke pattern, converging on identifiable centres, the discovery in itself does not reveal the ends which they served. The principal purposes currently proposed are related to ritual walking, to water supplies, and to the division of the territory into clear strips.

While Aveni himself insists that the lines were intended to be walked along, the people of the pampa would have had to have been indefatigable walkers to require 762 lines for mere peregrination, though Cahuachi was undoubtedly an important place of pilgrimage, to judge by its material remains. Equally, the use of the lines to serve as divisional boundaries may seem questionable, due to their extreme complexity.

Some connection of the lines with the quest for water would seem logical, in view of the stress laid by Aveni and others on the fact that water constitutes the most important commodity in the Nazca community. The pampa is bordered by two tributaries of the Río Grande, the Río Ingenio and the Río Nazca; gulleys cutting across the pampa drain water from the high Andes into this narrow strip, lying between the Andes and the Pacific Ocean, where it almost never rains, a process in the course of which the precious liquid plummets from 3000 metres to sea level. Many lines on close examination appear to have been established along the two rivers and their tributaries that pass from the mountains on to the pampa. A number of lines converged on centres that seem to have been deliberately located within view of tributaries that connect the main pampa with the river valleys; for reasons that are not altogether clear, such centres are tied exclusively to the Río Nazca, including those located nearer to the Río Ingenio lying to the north of the lines. There is a high concentration of centres on the north bank of the Río Nazca immediately opposite Cahuachi.

Somewhat paradoxically, though ethnographic studies of the region suggest that Cerro Blanco (elevation 2078 metres), visible from much of the pampa, was important in local rites for inducing the rains, and was worshipped as a means of providing water, from centres situated nearest to Cerro Blanco not a single line is orientated to within five degrees of that peak. None the less, Aveni, having studied in great detail other possibilities, including explanations based on astronomy, adheres to the view that while the evidence may as yet be far from conclusive, the one dominant commodity that correlates with his data on the focal line centres is water, so vital to the region. The location of all sixty-two line centres along the major rivers or very near to tributaries is far too consistent to be coincidental.

Further Comparisons

The temptation may arise to view the Nazca lines as a unique phenomenon, without comparison in Peru or elsewhere. But, as we have seen above, Alfred Métraux, working in Bolivia in 1934, had already discovered pathways leading up to countless small shrines made by the Chipaya Indians; he described such pathways as converging on isolated shrines like spokes on a wheel, somewhat recalling Aveni's mapping of the Nazca lines. One may equally mention Reinhard's discovery of a comparable phenomenon in the north Chilean desert.

Aveni even draws attention to parallels between the Nazca lines and the long straight roads that radiated from the Inca capital, Cuzco. Inexplicably certain of these roads suddenly widened, changed course and assumed a partially trapezoid form.

Comparisons have also been proposed between the lines and the Inca *ceque* system (*ceque* is the Quechua word for line). According to the chronicler Bernabé Cobo, the *ceque* system of Cuzco consisted of four lines or *ceques* radiating from the Temple of the Sun in Cuzco; along these *ceques* 328 holy sites, or *huacas*, were situated. Tom Zuidema, who spent many years of research on the subject, states that the majority of the *ceques* were not actual pathways, and could not be clearly identified on the ground. Rather, the Incas conceived them as invisible connections between these sacred *huacas* scattered along their length, but often not precisely situated on the straight course of a line. However, *ceques* were also connected with certain forms of human sacrifice, and victims, particularly children, were compelled to follow a straight line traced for the purpose along the course of a *ceque* to reach their place of sacrifice. It is important also to note that certain other *ceques* clearly do not begin at the Temple of the Sun in Cuzco, and hence in a sense more than one unified system existed.

The 328 *huacas*, according to Zuidema's interpretation, consisted of temples, arrangements of stones, or even certain trees; it is most significant that some were connected with springs and other natural wells; in many cases the water theme and its association with the Inca agricultural calendar is much in evidence. For instance, one *ceque* of the Chinchasuyu quadrant of Cuzco, known as Sucana, was a hill by way of which the water channel from Chinchero reached the city. Other *ceque* lines were associated with bends in rivers, and certain rituals associated with the *ceque* system stress the relationship between people and water.

The *ceque* system in its turn has been compared with the image of the *quipu*, the use of which served as a substitute for writing as a means of keeping records, used by the Incas and certain other Andean peoples. The *quipu* consisted of a thick cotton cord from which were suspended many thinner cords, each containing clusters of knots. If a *quipu* is spread out on a flat surface it can easily be noted that it resembles the plan of the *ceques*, since the cords of the *quipu* radiate outwards in every direction, like the *ceque* lines. The *quipu* was fundamental to the whole system of control of the Inca Empire, as we shall later see, and though we cannot now interpret the surviving *quipus*, the records confirm that they were able to register an almost incredible amount of data.

The Unsolved Mystery

As Johann Reinhard rightly observes, the vast pattern of Nazca lines, trapezoids and geoglyphs captures our attention above all because no simple explanations exist as to their origins or purpose. Probably we shall never reach a precise conclusion as to their meaning, or to the purpose that they served; they could even have had uses of which we are totally unaware.

Further research may help to clarify the general problem and the many unanswered questions that arise. For instance, the prehistoric climate of the Nazca region is still poorly known at the present time. Equally, opinions still differ as to whether the lines and the geoglyphs are contemporary, or belong to two different cultural horizons.

Persis Clarkson, as we have seen, is convinced that the geoglyphs are not necessarily contemporary with the basic Nazca culture, generally associated with the lines, and discusses the possibility that they might belong more to the following period, the Middle Horizon, which began in about AD 600, though relatively few shards from that era have been found in their vicinity. At all events, it would seem that the creation of all the lines and glyphs was extended over a long period of time. It should be added that Nazca itself, distinguished for its pottery, continued to retain a certain significance as a major supplier of cotton for textiles.

While the astronomic significance of the lines now tends to be discounted, Avéni, Urton and others have argued cogently that they were closely connected with rites associated with the crucial importance of water supplies, and that, as such, were meant to be trod upon.

Parallels exist in other civilizations. The ancient Egyptians climbed up on to the dry desert to conduct specific rituals. But the Nazca lines are essentially a part of a continuous trait of Andean cultures, in which a mystical devotion to patterns of straight lines, found also in the deserts of Bolivia and Chile, is deep-rooted and played a role that has no precise comparison in other parts of the globe.

Far from being a practice confined to a particular era or region, the linear concept can thus be seen as a notable feature of pre-Hispanic Andean culture. The Inca road system might even be cited as relevant to this concept, involving in some cases the expansion of roads built in the Nazca area long before.

CHAPTER FOUR

THE MIDDLE KINGDOMS

Tiahuanaco

As the basically maritime Moche era drew to its close, a new culture came to the fore in highland Peru, mainly centred upon the Valley of Ayacucho, lying about 500 kilometres south-east of Lima, and whose principal site is Huari; its iconography is closely linked to that of Tiahuanaco, on the southern shore of Lake Titicaca, in what is now part of Bolivia. Its period of ascendancy, now known as the Middle Horizon, lasted from approximately AD 600 to 1000.

Unquestionably Tiahuanaco has a longer history than Huari, and is, therefore, best considered first. In contrast to the more conservative chronology now generally accepted of Tiahuanaco's apogee as a major centre during the Middle Horizon, certain earlier writers reached ambitious conclusions. Some insisted that Tiahuanaco was a flourishing city aeons before the Christian era. In 1875 a distinguished Bolivian linguist even claimed that the Aymara language was the earliest human tongue and that Tiahuanaco, where Aymara was spoken, was therefore the world's oldest city.

Such views had an irresistible appeal for Erich von Däniken, the tireless inventor of theories on the origins of American man.

Von Däniken describes his 'detailed research' at Tiahuanaco and proposed a date of 600 BC for its main buildings, since the Prophet Ezekiel's encounter with a spaceship took place in 592 BC, an event that supported his conclusion that extraterrestrial spacemen set up a base at Tiahuanaco. Supposedly they brought no building materials but used their own special tools to erect its fabulous buildings.

This notion may have been indirectly inspired by certain observations of the chronicler Cieza de León, who visited the site in the mid-1550s. Cieza first remarks that Tiahuanaco was not a very large town, though famous for its great buildings, which were a remarkable thing to behold. Cieza affirms that he could not fathom what tools were used to work the huge gateway monument, and further suggests that the site was the oldest antiquity in Peru. Indeed the stonework of Tiahuanaco is, at least until Inca times, the finest in all the Andes; stones are fitted together with insets and tenons, bound with copper clamps.

Even wilder fantasies about the supposed origins of Tiahuanaco derived from H. S. Bellamy, a disciple of the Austrian Hans Horbiger, whose system of 'glacial cosmology' was based on the notion that the Earth had possessed several other moons before the present one. These had originally been independent planets, orbiting the sun somewhere between Earth and Mars. One by one these captive bodies crashed upon Earth with cataclysmic consequences; after each disaster, some great civilization perished.

Horbiger's theories about Earth's many former moons were taken up by Bellamy, who in 1943 published a book, *Built Before the Flood*, insisting that Tiahuanaco had flourished since time immemorial and that the original city was devastated when one of Horbiger's moons crashed upon Earth's surface.

Rejecting as absurd the notion that Tiahuanaco could ever have been built at an altitude of over 4000 metres, Bellamy maintained that following the first disaster, the site was refounded on land which then stood at sea level; this state prevailed because, after the Earth was shorn of the first of its other satellites, the present moon, following its triumphant survival, adopted an eccentric course, swinging round the Earth's globe three times in every forty-eight hours. Its speed and proximity drew off all the waters into equatorial regions, and as a result almost all South America was flooded. Hence the present Tiahuanaco was built at sea level on an island refuge in the midst of the ocean that had submerged the whole continent. About 13,000 years after the building of this second Tiahuanaco, consisting of the ruins visible today, the sea sank, and the surrounding territory was left high and dry, except for the present-day lake of Titicaca.

The legend of Tiahuanaco's immense antiquity was cited by other Spanish chroniclers in addition to Cieza. Writing nearly a century later,

Bernabé Cobo told of a legend (which he describes as a 'foolish tale') that the creator god made all things in Tiahuanaco, where he supposedly resided.

Tiahuanaco, because of its awesome altitude, enthrals all who favour bizarre accounts of America's origins, and they are drawn to this site as bees to honey. Bellamy is thus one of several who, in order to support notions of its immense antiquity, also devised complex calendric interpretations of the symbols carved on Tiahuanaco's most famous monument, known as the Gate of the Sun. At the basis of all this pseudo-science lies the notion that humans simply could not have built the site at its present altitude; it was taken for granted that the great blocks of stone, visible today, could not have been dragged to their present location by human hands, so great would have been the effort required to work at this level above the sea.

Such authors, however, tend to forget that the effects of altitude are very relative. Modern searchers after occult messages drawn from the ruins obviously puff and blow when they descend from their vehicles and breathe the rarefied air of the Bolivian *altiplano*. (I myself once drove from nearby La Paz in a taxi to beyond a stone indicating an altitude of 4500 metres; all I could do was to crawl from the taxi, throw one snowball at the driver, and return!) But it becomes easy to overlook the fact that Indians who live near Lake Titicaca today are naturally adapted to such heights and moreover their bodies do not function so well at sea level. In a mining village called Totoral, south of Cuzco, situated at an altitude of 4800 metres, football is played with enthusiasm and in nearby La Paz, situated only slightly lower than Tiahuanaco, every form of manual labour is performed in a perfectly routine manner!

It may be added that even Arthur Posnansky, who published much invaluable data on the site of Tiahuanaco in the 1940s, nevertheless clung to the notion that it had been built fourteen to fifteen thousand years ago! However, as we shall see, researchers have today reached more prosaic conclusions. None the less they, like their more imaginative predecessors, are naturally impressed by the grandeur of the site, built at such an altitude. Moreover, these vestiges of former splendour had already impressed both the Incas and their Spanish conquerors; Bernabé Cobo relates that the Inca emperor Pachacutec was so amazed at the stonework of such structures, unlike anything that he had ever seen before, that he commanded his men to take careful note of how they were erected, for he wanted his own capital, Cuzco, to be rebuilt in the same fashion.

Modern Research

In terms of modern research, an initial phase for the site of Pucara, which lies to the north of Lake Titicaca, indeed dates from about 200 BC; Pucara unquestionably influenced Tiahuanaco, whose elaborate Chiripa pottery is of comparable antiquity. Many of Tiahuanaco's principal monuments were probably erected in the early centuries of our era, during the period now known as Tiahuanaco III. They therefore preceded the 'Expansive' stage of Tiahuanaco which has a distinctive religious iconography, closely related to the Peruvian Middle Horizon (AD 600–1000) in Huari and elsewhere. While the Tiahuanaco that we see today is more contemporary with, say, Byzantine than with early Egyptian structures, it is none the less imposing.

On the one side the site commands a view over the bleak *altiplano*, surrounded by snow-capped peaks; in the opposite direction, to the north-west, lies the great expanse of Lake Titicaca, some twenty kilometres distant; while the ruins, suggestive of an original city of imposing grandeur, are situated 100 metres higher than the water and command a fine view of Lake Titicaca. The latter is nowadays perhaps best seen from the air, from where one can admire the vast extent of its deep turquoise waters.

Tiahuanaco is such an impressive site that, quite apart from the more exotic forms of speculation described above, it began to attract scholars at an early date. The German archaeologists Alfons Stubel and Max Uhle published an extensive monograph in 1892. They were among the first to establish a basic cultural timedepth in the Andean area by demonstrating that the sculptural art of Tiahuanaco was older than that of the Incas. Subsequently many other archaeologists worked at Tiahuanaco, such as Wendell Bennett in 1934 and Alfred Kidder in 1956. Since then, extensive research has been conducted by Carlos Ponce.

The site of Tiahuanaco, measuring approximately 1000 by 500 metres, as originally mapped by Posnansky, constitutes the first planned monumental city of South America. More recent excavations have revealed an urban zone occupying an area of about four square kilometres. The core area of the city contains the imposing pyramid of Akapana and the better-known sunken temple, Kalasaya. Nearby stands the famous Gate of the Sun. Carved upon it is the best-known example of the basic iconographic theme of the Middle Horizon, the staffed front-face deity flanked by profile attendants, which also appears, as we shall see, in highland Peru and even in ceremonial urns from the coast.

Carlos Ponce suggests that the monumental temples were built some

Figure 18 Frieze of Weeping Sun God

time before AD 300. It was only in the subsequent period (according to a series of radiocarbon dates beginning in about AD 600, though certain authors prefer a somewhat later date) that what became the typical Tiahuanaco iconography was adopted; the temples which had originally borne no images of this front-face deity were then refurbished with façades and sculptures replete with such figures; these included the Gate of the Sun. Of this iconography, of which the frieze of the Gate of the Sun is fairly typical, the exact origins are unknown. This frieze consists of the sun god, who holds two staffs adorned with puma and condor heads. He sheds a kind of zoomorphic tears, the form of which varied as the theme spread to highland Peru. The central god is flanked by figures with staffs in their hands and furled wings.

Figure 19 Figures Which Flank the Tiahuanaco Sun God

In terms of chronology for this Tiahuanaco iconography, also adapted at sites in central Peru, objects from Pucara form at least some antecedent; their basic theme presents strange-looking versions of a front-faced deity surrounded by attendants very similar to those found in later variants. Radiocarbon dates for these Pucara images cluster in the first century BC. The site must have survived for several centuries, but William Isbell suspects that some other possible ancestor of the typical Tiahuanacoid iconography may exist, perhaps in the little-known area between Lake Titicaca and the Amazonic jungle.

Figure 20 Tiahuanaco Drinking Vessel

Huari

At the time when Tiahuanaco stood at its apogee, in the second half of the first millennium, a leading centre situated far to the north-west in highland Peru was Huari, which lies on the eastern edge of the Valley of Ayacucho, at between 2700 and 3100 metres above sea level. Though they share a common iconography, the ruins of Huari, much less well preserved, failed to impress the Spaniards like those of Tiahuanaco; none the less, the indefatigable observer Cieza de León visited the area in the mid-sixteenth century, and reported large and ancient buildings on the Río Vinaque, clearly identifiable with the site of Huari. 'Their dilapidated and ruined condition indicates that they have stood for many ages. Asking the local Indians who built the ancient constructions, they answer that another people, bearded and light-skinned like the Spaniards, came to these lands long before the Incas reigned, and built here their dwellings.' Cieza further notes that such buildings were generally square, whereas those of the Incas were long and narrow.

*Figure 21 Huari Drinking Vessel Also Illustrating Weeping Deity Similar to
Those of Tiahuanaco*

Huari embraces an area of at least fifteen square kilometres; it is not
only high but dry, and has no natural water supply. The core of the
site contains many stone buildings; only one Early Horizon structure has
been identified and the remainder correspond to the Middle Horizon.
Notwithstanding its evident relationship to Tiahuanaco, some earlier
visitors, such as the German Disselhof, insist that certain aspects of its
culture also derived from Nazca.

Huari was built on no preconceived plan, but developed in a more dramatic fashion after megalithic dressed stone, so characteristic of Tiahuanaco, had made its first appearance in Huari in the initial stages of the
Middle Horizon, probably between A D 550 and 600. Estimates of population vary widely, ranging from a total of 70,000 to as low as 20,000.

After Cieza's visit in about 1550, the site received little attention
until Julio Tello visited the Valley of Ayacucho in 1942. Richard
Schaedel in 1948 published excellent photographs of Huari stone statues
and in 1950 Wendell Bennett conducted a season of excavation. In the

1960s, Luis Lumbreras and Dorothy Menzel made further studies, and raised the question, still unresolved by more recent investigations, as to whether Huari was the capital of a conquest state.

Characteristic of Huari architecture are the walled compounds. These compounds are divided into rectangular sections consisting of patios, surrounded by a number of rooms. They may have been family residences of a rather barrack-like nature, since some contain kitchens.

Archaeological evidence points to three distinct stages in Huari architecture. In the first phase of its existence, before the walled compounds, a number of temples had been constructed at Huari, which then became both a ceremonial and a residential city. One temple provided a carbon date of A D 580 ± 60. These earlier temples were built of dressed stone, a form of construction later abandoned; dressed-stone chambers were also found in Cheqo Wasi, a site at the southern extremity of the Huari urban area.

The second phase, that of the walled compounds, also described as the Patio Group Construction Phase, was more prolonged, and most of the city's core was occupied during this period. At this time marked differences are evident between the northern and southern halves of the site, suggesting some form of dual division of the community. The Mora-duchayuq Compound in the centre of Huari is the best-known example of Patio Group architecture. Spatial organization within the compounds was very regular, the rooms and patios being connected by doorways. This Patio Group phase in the architecture in northern Huari seems to have been organized around a pair of intersecting avenues. Access is limited to a main entrance in the west wall and three secondary entrances in further stretches of the wall. The compound is composed of at least seven almost identical clusters of rooms, or patio groups.

Many artefacts were unearthed that suggest that the compound might have served as a high-class residence. Not only is the proportion of serving vessels, bowls and cups, higher than what might be normal for ordinary domestic use, but in addition many wide-mouthed jars were found, used for the storage and fermentation of the ritual *chicha*. The nature of the remains suggests that the occupants gave feasts, and hence that they belonged to the administrative class. In addition, the compound yielded a high percentage of elaborate ceramics, as well as imported luxury items such as spondylus shells. Nearly all the artefacts are finished

products, and tools normally associated with agriculture or with manu-
facturing were notable by their absence.

In the latter stage of the existence of Huari some of its buildings
were apparently razed to make way for a dramatic reconstruction. The
most impressive remains of this third phase that survive in Huari today
are buildings of monumental proportions with higher walls that were
never finished before the city was mysteriously abandoned. William
Isbell defines this development as the Great Walls Construction Phase,
though such construction ceased before its buildings were completed.
The latter are hard to classify as residential quarters and walled streets
have not been identified; any equivalent is, moreover, absent in other
sites of the same period.

The southern part of the Huari site differs in many respects from the
northern sector of the city described above. Not only are the buildings
more poorly preserved, the walls are so badly destroyed that they are
hard to identify. Moreover, the buildings of southern Huari are much
smaller than those in the northern part. Such constructions also belong
basically to the Patio Group phase.

While it is thus possible to describe the impressive, if ill-preserved,
site of Huari in terms of its three phases of development, it becomes
much harder, in the total absence of written traditions, to offer an
interpretation of its true significance. The question arises as to how far
the ruling, or administrative, Huari class, as tentatively described above,
held sway merely over the city, over a state comprising some nearby
centres, or even over a much more extensive empire. Also relevant to
such problems are Huari relations with Tiahuanaco in its later phases
and the obvious significance of the distinctive iconography shared by
the two centres. However, before broaching such questions, the more
salient features of certain other sites of the same period must first be
considered.

Nearby Sites

Throughout the Peruvian Andes other sites have been excavated, whose
architecture and pottery in varying degree recall those of Huari itself.
Some scholars, as we shall later see, refer to such sites as Huari provincial

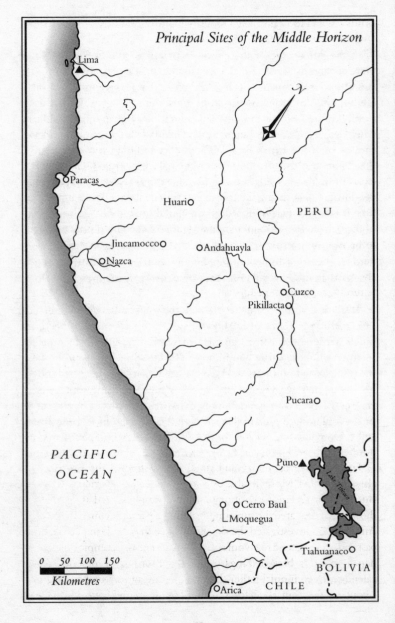

Principal Sites of the Middle Horizon

N

Lima

Paracas

Huari

Jincamocco

Nazca

Andahuayla

PERU

Cuzco

Pikillacta

Pucara

PACIFIC
OCEAN

Puno

Lake Titicaca

Cerro Baul

Moquegua

Tiahuanaco

0   50   100 150

Kilometres

BOLIVIA

Arica

CHILE

centres. Those situated, like Huari itself, in the Valley of Ayacucho are among the most relevant. After Huari, one of the most important is Conchopata, in which Julio Tello in 1942 found oversize pottery urns with polychrome icons very similar to those of some statues at Tiahuanaco. These are often regarded as the earliest example of a shared iconography between Tiahuanaco and Huari.

Conchopata lies on the outskirts of the modern Ayacucho, about ten kilometres distant as the crow flies from Huari; it is significant more for its artefacts and pottery, related to those of Huari and Tiahuanaco, than for its architecture, most of which has been destroyed. More recent excavations have established that Conchopata was already occupied in pre-Huari times during the fourth and fifth centuries of our era; at this time it was stylistically related to the Nazca region. Unlike other sites of the period, the structures are not typical of the Huari plan and seem to be more suggestive of a rural settlement that grew according to its needs. Ceramic production was abundant; it is likely that metal was also worked and that long-distance trade included luxury goods, such as turquoise, gold and copper.

Another Valley of Ayacucho site, Azángaro, is situated about fifteen kilometres north-west of Huari. Most of its ruins present an image of grid-like regularity. They comprise a rectangular enclosure which covers an area of eight hectares, divided into three distinctive sectors. Throughout the work carried out on the site, many unexpected features emerged. The north sector contains spacious rectangular enclosures, typical of Huari construction. In contrast, the central sector consists of forty rows of much smaller rooms, while the southern sector again consists of courts and galleries, but less regular in construction than those of the northern sector.

The presence of luxury and ritual goods stressed the existence of class differences. More notable by their presence were agricultural tools. But Azángaro seems too elaborate to have simply served as a home for those who cultivated the surrounding fields, a paradox which led Martha Anders, who investigated the site, to observe that Andean people, both past and present, tend to favour structures that convey complex messages; hence, on this basis, Azángaro may be more aptly described as a calendrical-ceremonial rather than as a merely agricultural centre. The layout of the central sector suggests that it might have served as a precedent for the elaborate ritual of the shrines of Inca Cuzco. Abandoned at the end of the Middle Horizon, radiocarbon dates cluster round its later years, ranging from A D 760 to 990.

Outstanding among Huari period sites is Pikillacta, located to the south-east of Cuzco in the Río Lucre basin at the southern end of the Valley of Cuzco.

It was not until 1959 that a ground plan of Pikillacta was published, at a time when it was still assumed that this was an Inca site. William Sanders conducted the first excavations in the 1960s; he discovered few artefacts, but correctly concluded that it belonged to the Huari rather than to the Inca culture. Since 1982 Gordon McEwan has carried out detailed excavations and provided copious information on the site.

It soon became apparent that Pikillacta was not an isolated Huari stronghold, but one of several fairly large sites lying within and around the Lucre basin; each occupies one of the five entrances to the basin, of which the site of Pikillacta itself was the nerve centre.

The salient architectural feature of Pikillacta is a huge rectangular enclosure that measures 745 by 630 metres. On each side of this massive block are several other enclosures; in all the site thus covers an area of about two square kilometres. Pikillacta was essentially a planned city. McEwan's structural survey revealed the rather surprising fact that the walls that formed the perimeter of the site were built first as a structural shell for a preplanned master project; since subterranean canals were also built as part of this project, the plan must have been very detailed.

Pikillacta, originally conceived by Sanders more as a kind of Huari frontier garrison, McEwan now describes as a major residential centre. The excavations yielded as many as 18,000 potsherds and 25,000 bones and bone fragments, together with a fairly massive store of artefacts; radiocarbon dates for some of these range between A D 500 and 600. Data so far available make it hard to estimate the total population. McEwan suggests that the two basic functions of the site were residential and ceremonial; these would have been dependent upon a third function, administration, which might have been the original purpose of its planned construction, if indeed it formed part of any extensive Huari-dominated domain.

The Northern Middle Horizon

In contrast to nearby Azángaro and Pikillacta, the Huari-era sites of Huamachuco and Viracochapampa lie far to the north-west of Huari. Viracochapampa is less than four kilometres north of the modern town of Huamachuco. It consists of a series of rectangular buildings typical of Huari-period sites. Grouped around a central plaza, many of these are niched halls, i.e. large buildings surrounded by solid walls containing many rows of niches. The exact purpose served by such niches is not altogether clear; since niches weaken the walls, these halls are often poorly preserved. In all, nineteen niched halls have been mapped.

Viracochapampa was apparently never completed. Substantial evidence exists for this assumption: a canal system beneath the floors of buildings was never connected; plaster floors were not laid; and in some cases temporary masonry supports for the lintels of doors and large niches were never removed. In addition, the boundary wall of the site was unfinished.

Other sites of the same period exist in the vicinity of Huamachuco. A complex of buildings identified as round storerooms was found at Cerro Amaru. They are constructed on raised floors with ventilation below, suggesting the storage of seed crops, a hypothesis confirmed by evidence that maize was kept in these structures. After a period of use these storerooms were burnt and their shells remodelled into apparently domestic dwellings. Two charcoal samples were dated to AD 400 and 680. A mausoleum was also found at Cerro Amaru that contained a plentiful store of pottery. All of this can be dated to the Middle Horizon, and much can be identified with the iconography of Huari, though other ceramics display the influence of the Pacific coast, as well as of Cajamarca. In addition, spondylus shells, obsidian and lapis lazuli have been found. Spondylus shells were brought mainly from Ecuador and the lapis lazuli more probably derived from the Cuzco region.

Niched halls were also common in another nearby site, Marca Huamachuco, apparently built over a period of 500 years, embracing approximately the whole Middle Horizon. Marca Huamachuco is the largest known Huari-period site in northern Peru. Unlike most others, so strictly rectangular, its ruins include curvilinear galleries. Like some of the buildings of Cerro Amaru, their origins are pre-Huari with construction beginning before AD 400.

As we shall later see, the relationship between Huari and the Huamachuco sites is not easy to define. Like Pikillacta, Viracochapampa was a planned site, though its planning was perhaps less rigid. An exact chronology is hard to establish and the interesting question arises as to whether the galleries and niched halls, also present in Huari and Pikillacta, might not have first originated in the Huamachuco sites; Viracochapampa, which was never finished, was perhaps one of the first provincial centres to be planned and built. While Huari architectural traits are notable, many Huamachuco sites lack Huari ceramics. Only a few have been found at Viracochapampa, though at Cerro Amaru they are more plentiful.

John Topic describes the relationship between Huari and Huamachuco as brief but intense. At Cerro Amaru the archaeological evidence points to the importance of trade with southern Peru, and commerce may have been crucial to the relationship with Huari. The more recent evidence equally suggests that another site, Marca Huamachuco (where construction began before AD 600), thrived during and after the period suggestive of a Huari presence.

Yet further to the north certain fairly important sites flourished at the outset of the Middle Horizon. The most notable of these are Pampa Grande, on the Río Lambayeque about forty kilometres inland, and Galindo, south-west of Cajamarca, lying on the Río Moche. In Cajamarca itself, Huari shards are rare, and a Huari presence is not well documented. However, at least trade relations existed between the two regions, since many Cajamarca-style pieces have been found at sites in the Valley of Ayacucho.

Pampa Grande, which flourished between AD 600 and 700, displays certain Huari influences but belongs basically to Moche V, the transitional phase corresponding to a time when the earlier Moche sites had already been abandoned. It seems to have been the short-lived capital of a major north-coast polity. Moche V iconography, as we have seen in Chapter 2, marks a fairly radical departure from that of its forerunners; unlike these, Moche V, while retaining certain traditional deities, lays much stress on maritime activities, and the boat made of rushes there becomes a current art form.

Galindo, some 160 kilometres to the south of Pampa Grande, is a much smaller site also corresponding in time to the early Middle Horizon and Moche V pottery was also found at the site. Unlike Pampa Grande, Galindo was heavily fortified, with complex defensive walls that run for more than a kilometre, together with evidence of repair and reconstruction. The site might be viewed in one particular sense as a precursor of Chan Chan, the mighty kingdom that, as we shall see, thrived in coastal Peru in post-Huari times; a structure closely resembling the great palace enclosures of Chan Chan has been found at Galindo. It is the Galindo walls that are more striking than its monuments; such fortifications found in this region led to previous assumptions of a possible Huari conquest. However, the Río Moche Valley contains no remains remotely resembling those of Huari. The defences at Galindo are no longer therefore seen as a response to such a distant threat and any true Huari presence so far to the north tends to be discounted.

State or Empire

The Middle Horizon continues to puzzle those who attempt to interpret its essence. But before trying to define the respective roles in the Middle Horizon of Huari and Tiahuanaco, the two leading centres of the period, indisputably linked by a shared iconography, the question first arises: what was the relationship between Huari and the various Huari-period sites outlined above? How far, if at all, did Huari extend its control beyond the bounds of the city itself?

During the 1950s, when Huari stylistic influence on the Peruvian north coast was noted by Larco-Hoyle and others, this led to the assumption that such influence might derive from Huari military conquest. In the 1960s, Luis Lumbreras described Huari as an empire, and Dorothy Menzel in her study of Middle Horizon ceramics concluded that Huari might be seen as the capital of an extended conquest state. This viewpoint was tentatively shared by other leading scholars, and in the 1960s the theory of military expansion as the key to the spread of Huari influences was widely accepted.

During the 1980s, William Isbell and others have continued to grapple with the question as to how far Huari might have achieved conquests beyond the Valley of Ayacucho. The militaristic nature of Huari town planning with its grim walled enclosures might suggest such conclusions; what has been aptly described as the sense of jail or concentration camp hangs eerily over the repetitive cellular portions of Huari site plans. One may point, moreover, to the rigid division of classes evident in Azángaro, or to the walls with limited access that divide different sectors of this and other sites. In Huari itself high walls cut off whole districts of the city and it becomes hard to envision how people could even move from one sector to another.

However, in recent years many scholars tend to interpret the Peruvian Middle Horizon more as an era of independent regional centres and to argue that the extent of any Huari conquest may at times have been exaggerated. They further suggest that a number of independent polities existed during the period and that Huari–Tiahuanacoid iconography found throughout the central Andes was spread more by commercial contact and shared religious beliefs, rather than by sheer conquest. Such views were in part influenced by studies of coastal Peru. Whereas Max Uhle as early as 1896 wrote of close ties between the style of Pachacamac, a large site to the south of present-day Lima, and Tiahuanaco, coastal conquests by both Tiahuanaco and Huari have since been largely discounted. Moreover, notions of any Huari conquest of coastal Peru, to the north of the Río Moche, should now also be excluded; recent work at sites originally linked with Huari on the evidence of scanty ceramic remains shows that such centres are either of much later date or, like Chan Chan, were based on local traditions. While finds of Huari-style ceramics may suggest that Huari had a certain impact on late Moche society, evidence of military conquest is virtually non-existent.

In considering Middle Horizon sites nearer to Huari itself, the notion of some kind of unified state becomes more plausible, though not easy to prove. The group of sites in the vicinity of the modern Huamachuco does display certain traits typical of Huari itself: for example, the division into large rectangular walled enclosures, some of which served as rather austere residences for numerous families. Viracochapampa is notable for its niched halls, and for the apparent fact that it was never completed, hardly proof of a long and stable submission to a Huari state. Niched halls also are found at Marca Huamachuco, but these and other Huari-type buildings in this site belong mainly to the earlier stages of its construction.

Huari ceramics occur at few sites in the Huamachuco region, but their relationship to Huari itself, if intense, seems to have been rather brief. The role, if any, of military coercion remains unclear; the question might be better understood if trade relations could be more closely defined; evidence exists as to the presence in Huamachuco of goods from the south as well as from the north, but the mechanisms of exchange are at present hard to determine.

Pikillacta, nearer to Huari itself, certainly displays Huari features, and radiocarbon dates from the site cover almost the total duration of the Middle Horizon. Like Viracochapampa, another planned city, walls are everywhere in evidence; not only does Pikillacta have a perimeter wall, built before the town, but walls also serve as divisions between structures and as boundaries between structures and avenues. If the functions of Pikillacta are indeed mainly residential and ceremonial, administration may have been its principal role, perhaps under the auspices of Huari itself.

Tiahuanaco and Huari

The broader implications of the relationship between the two polities, linked by a common iconography, involve one further site, Moquegua, situated far to the south of Huari, together with its neighbour, the hilltop site of Cerro Baul.

In all, a cluster of nine archaeological sites has been studied in the Moquegua Valley. Most of these, except for Cerro Baul, seem to have been associated more with Tiahuanaco than with Huari. In several locations decorated wares have been unearthed that are virtually indistinguishable from those of Tiahuanaco's final phase. In one huge cemetery at Chan Chan ceramics display the more typical Tiahuanaco traits, such as the stylized flamingo, together with certain geometric designs; Chan Chan pottery in Moquegua is even to be compared with that of far-off Tiahuanaco outposts, such as Cochabamba.

In marked contrast, in Cerro Baul, built on a steep nearby hill, far from resembling the local Tiahuanaco-type centres of the valley below, the monumental architecture at the summit is more comparable to that of Pikillacta, and of Huari itself. In addition, Cerro Baul pottery, quite distinct from that of Tiahuanaco, recalls in every detail the style of the earlier phases of Huari expansion.

Since the investigation of Cerro Baul is far from complete, it becomes difficult to offer even a tentative explanation of how and why it differs so much in style and form from its neighbours. None the less data from the Moquegua Valley demonstrate that Huari influences extended as far south, while Tiahuanaco's cultural penetration also stretched westwards to this location.

In studying relations between Tiahuanaco and Huari, chronological problems are significant. The great Tiahuanaco site undoubtedly existed long before the construction of Huari itself and of other Huari-era sites in Peru. The view of Tiahuanaco as the source of Middle Horizon iconography and as the dominant power during that period is emphatically expressed by the Bolivian archaeologist Carlos Ponce. Many other scholars, however, insist that the evidence from Tiahuanaco does not confirm the belief that their shared iconography was present in that site long before it appeared in the Huari area.

It has been argued that the origins of the iconography later present in Huari and Tiahuanaco (but not in the earliest phases of the latter) seem to have derived from Pucara, whose origins go back to about 200 BC. Earlier pottery from Tiahuanaco seems to have also been much influenced by certain coastal wares first discovered by Max Uhle in 1896 at Pachacamac. This hybrid style was then known as Coast Tiahuanaco.

It was not until some time after AD 500 that monuments of Tiahuanaco, which had already existed for centuries, were then refurbished and thereafter bore the symbols of the distinctive Middle Horizon iconography, depicting the staffed front-face deity, present in both Huari and Tiahuanaco sites. Previous to this renewal, Tiahuanaco stone sculpture was mainly decorated with reptilian and feline figures that survived from earlier periods.

While this central deity theme pattern was adopted both in Huari and Tiahuanaco, it becomes hard to determine that it derived either from one or the other of the two sites. Though iconographic details may vary from place to place, the main components consist of staffed front-face deities flanked by profile attendants and other human figures. The medium of expression varies; in Tiahuanaco the theme is presented above all on the great stone sculptures. In Huari it appears mainly on pottery, more particularly on huge ritual jars and urns; it is also displayed on wooden spoons with decorated handles. Miniature stone artefacts were also produced in Huari.

The typical Tiahuanaco—Huari iconographic images include both human and supernatural beings. The staffed front-face figure and his profile attendants display supernatural traits. The profile attendants face each other; while their features are human, small trophy heads are often found around their eyes and chins. They bear a staff in the left hand, an axe and trophy head in the right, a feature which has earned them the epithet of 'sacrificer'. They are depicted in profile and usually have one leg forward and the other to the back as though either kneeling or running. Some of these attendants are winged, elaborately dressed and wear head-dresses not unlike that of the front-face deity himself. It should be added that the notion of a front-face deity is a very ancient Andean symbol and was already widespread during the Chavin era.

Of the staffed front-face deity displayed in the architrave (the decorative beam that spans the opening) of the famous Gate of the Sun, the body is only partly visible. The head-dress is adorned with felines and the deity holds the symbolic staffs in each hand; tear motifs surround the eyes. No fewer than forty associated figures are represented; instead of floating horizontally, as in other instances, they are shown as running, with extended wings. The doorway and passage associated with the Gate of the Sun architrave seems to have been of the greatest symbolic importance. Tapestries and textiles found nearby bear a close similarity; moreover, the architrave and its gateway opening are often repeated in miniature form as an iconic device on other buildings. No known architraves date from the final phase at Tiahuanaco, but the theme survived on textiles and ceramics that were made long after the last architrave.

But while iconographic similarities between the two great Middle Horizon polities may be easy to identify, certain differences remain obvious. In the first phase, notwithstanding the apparent presence of some common beliefs, the leading feature of Tiahuanaco culture, shared by many sites in that region, was its stone sculpture, which was never transmitted to Huari. Stonework at Huari is not impressive, and stone sculpture is not a major component of the Valley of Ayacucho artistic tradition; even such monoliths as have been found are not typical of the Tiahuanaco style. Where stone was used it served different purposes; at Huari stone, for instance, served for certain burial chambers, but of a kind not found in Tiahuanaco.

Above all the architecture of the two polities is wholly different, both in form and concept. Only certain specific features appear in both; for instance, a sunken temple exists at Huari, but it is very different from those that are typical of Tiahuanaco both in style and layout. Equally, similarities exist between the methods of construction of Huari's buildings and of Tiahuanaco's massive stone structures and the technology of megalithic masonry in the two sites is surely related.

But it is above all in concept, as much as form, that the architecture of Tiahuanaco differs from that of Huari. As stressed above, Huari site plans convey an almost jail-like impression; for instance, Pikillacta consists of an endless series of rectangular enclosures and rooms whose design surprisingly suggests that they lacked identifiable doorways or entrances; at Azángaro the rectangular buildings of the north and south sectors of the site are divided by a continuous wall without gateways that provide access from one to the other. In contrast, at Tiahuanaco the architecture seems to be designed more to impress the onlooker and to convey meaning in a spiritual and civic sense; no grim walls divide the main buildings, whose purpose appears to be religious. While Huari architecture seems to lack formal entrances, Tiahuanaco has a long tradition of gateways and decorated portals, which probably served for large civic rituals. Both Tiahuanaco and Huari sites display a sense of geometry rather distinct from other Andean periods, but expressed in a fundamentally different manner. That of the former is horizontal, while in Huari's rectangular structures the concept is essentially vertical.

The nature of political or commercial links between the Tiahuanaco and Huari cultural zones is even harder to define. The presence of the latter in Cerro Baul has been ascribed to a Huari 'colonial intrusion' into a complex that contains Tiahuanaco-type administrative centres. But while reasons have been advanced to suggest that Huari was a conquest state, evidence at the moment is scarce of the occurrence of armed conflict between Huari and its southern neighbour. In the total absence of any written text, the silent stones tell us little. Military conquest often leaves few traces in the archaeological record, which tends to offer only rather scant evidence of sieges and battles leading to conquest.

Hence, in the present state of the available knowledge, Huari and Tiahuanaco may be conceived as forming integral parts of a well-defined chronological era, and as bearers of a common culture, but at the same time display differences that invite further study.

CHAPTER FIVE

THE GREAT CHIMOR

The Birth of Chimor

The kingdom of Chimor, prior to the rise of the Incas, came to dominate a long stretch of coastal Peru, extending from beyond Tumbez on the present-day Peruvian–Ecuadorian border to a point almost as far south as Lima, some 1000 kilometres distant. It is, therefore, the largest single realm in South America known to posterity before that of the Incas, to which it finally succumbed.

An account survives of the first ruler of Chimor: 'In this house he remained for the space of one year, performing the said ceremonies . . . With Indians whom he conquered he learned the language and they obeyed him and gave him their daughters. From that point he came to take the name of Chimor Capac (Chimor Lord). It is not known whence he came, except that . . . a great lord had sent him to govern this land from across the sea. The yellow powders which he used in his ceremonies and the cotton cloths which he used to cover his shameful parts are well known in these lands . . . This Taycanamu had a son called Guacricaur, who acquired more power than his father, conquering the Indians and important men in this valley.'

Thus begins the document known as the 'Anonymous History of Trujillo', written in 1604. Trujillo, which is situated some 800 kilometres north-west of Lima, lies adjacent to Chan Chan, the capital of the kingdom known as Chimor. Hence, in studying Chimor we are concerned with at least a proto-historical period in the story of ancient Peru, as compared with the grandiose but silent vestiges of its earlier phases, described in previous chapters. While its legendary past is thus immortalized in a few colonial documents, in recent decades Chimor has been the object of intense scientific research. In particular, a copious volume was published in 1990, recording a symposium held in Dumbarton Oaks that covered almost every aspect of the coastal kingdom, as studied by leading Andean scholars of today; some of these have sought to relate their findings to the somewhat fragmentary data derived from the surviving documents.

The realm of Chimor, as portrayed in the 'Anonymous History' and in the account of its northern provinces, written by the chronicler Cabello de Balboa, had already interested archaeologists since the nineteenth century, attracted by the vast hoard of pottery and metal artefacts yielded by its tombs, and above all by the spectacular palaces of the capital city of Chan Chan, so unique in size and structure.

It needs first to be stated that, unlike the realm of the Incas, Chimor was no pan-Peruvian empire and that other major polities flourished in the long era that spanned the end of the Huari–Tiahuanaco period in about AD 1000, and the rise of the Inca about 400 years later. This period is usually termed the Late Intermediate. Accounts also survive of the Aymara kingdoms of that era, in particular those of the Colla and Lupaqa located on the western side of Lake Titicaca, both of which produced distinctive styles of pottery. Conditions in the Bolivian Andes, following the decline of Tiahuanaco, seem to have remained unsettled; recent research suggests that much of the population forsook the shores of Lake Titicaca and retreated to the security of hilltop settlements, at heights above 4000 metres, ringed by defensive walls. Only after the Inca occupation several centuries later, were people induced to return to less harsh conditions.

In the Valley of Cuzco, the future Inca heartland, following the decline of the Huari centre of Pikillacta, smaller polities emerged that used a pottery known as Killke, while in the highlands to the north-east of Chimor, the inland kingdom of Cajamarca was already established. On the southern part of the Peruvian coast, never conquered by Chimor, the great shrine and oracle of Pachacamac flourished, as well as certain ancient polities which, as we shall later see, were among the first peoples to be conquered by the Incas.

Chimu Antecedents

Certain identifiable traits link the culture of Chimor to Huari, as well as to the last Moche phase, Moche V, and serve to illustrate the thread of continuity that runs through the successive Andean periods.

In Moche V, which, as we have seen in Chapter 2, followed the fall of the great monuments of the Huaca del Sol and the Huaca de la Luna, and the waning of the cult of the two-headed serpent, urbanism becomes more marked. Above all, north-coast art of Moche V represents a shift to marine motifs and to new marine deities, perhaps stressing the increased role of the ocean in their real world. The Moche double-headed serpent also survived in certain Chimu-period friezes on the north coast.

Other basic Moche elements may also be identified in Chimu art; for instance, monkeys, perched on the spouts of Chimu stirrup-spout bottles, can be traced back to those of Moche V. Galindo, the large ruins which lie almost within sight of the great Moche Huaca del Sol, was originally a Moche site, whose urban traits make it seem more like a true city, in itself a major change from the Huaca-dominated religious sites of the earlier Moche phases. The first palatial structure of a kind that became so characteristic of Chan Chan itself was erected at Galindo; it might be regarded as a Moche antecedent for the Chimu palaces.

Pampa Grande, further north at the neck of the Río Lambayeque, later conquered by Chimor, is also described as a Moche site that displays distinctly urban characteristics. Certain traces of a Huari influence are also present in Pampa Grande. At Batan Grande, another important Lambayeque site, a Moche V occupation underlies the ruins of the Chimu era.

At the same time, while such earlier influences may be identified, the emergence of Chan Chan represents in many respects a new departure. Though walls have a clear precedent in both Moche and Huari traditions, the immense dimensions of those that surrounded each of the Chan Chan palaces, often described as *ciudadelas*, were a new development; their scale may be interpreted as an expression of power and as the creation of a new image.

Early Beginnings

In contrast to the more allegorical version of events given by written sources, an increasing volume of concrete data is now provided by archaeological research. Monumental construction began in Chan Chan, situated in the Río Moche Valley, in about AD 850. Chan Chan was a place in which, unlike others, the parts were more important than the whole. The real unit was not the city itself but its ten great compounds or palaces, the *ciudadelas*.

In the early phase, to which the first three, or perhaps four, *ciudadelas* belong, expansion beyond Chan Chan itself was on a fairly modest scale. This phase, perhaps better described as basic consolidation, may have begun some time after AD 900 and continued until AD 1050; during this time the nearby Río Viru and Chicama Valleys probably became allied with or subject to the Chimu dynasty. Early Chimu pottery has been found in Cerro Lescano in the Río Chicama Valley, while in the Río Viru Valley such ceramics were also discovered, associated with walls and small structures.

Hence early Chimu expansion tended to be directed initially towards the more productive highlands rather than to coastal valleys. South of Tumbez, the coastland forms part of the driest New World desert, where annual precipitation at an altitude below about 1500 metres is almost negligible. Agriculture is dependent upon rivers that descend from the sierra; only later did Chimor come to dominate a majority of these large desert drainages, which are more abundant in the northern part of the Peruvian coast than further south.

The Fortifications Project of 1980 investigated this early inland advance. At Cerro de la Cruz, a site built about twenty kilometres inland in the Río Chao Valley, the project found evidence of a siege, and the presence of Chimu shards suggests that the invaders were Chimus. A Chimu fort, Cerro Coronado, was also built on the Río Chao about ten kilometres downstream towards the coast.

Traces of an early consolidation phase also survive in vestiges of fortifications at Cerro Galindo and Cerro Orejas, associated with early Chimu ceramics. These two sites are situated near the Río Moche at about seventeen kilometres inland. Also lying on the Río Moche, at another ten kilometres further from the sea, Cerro Pedregal probably marks the furthest advance inland made by the early Chimu; remains of an early wall, situated at 325 metres above sea level, served as a defence barrier, and perhaps as a frontier post.

Chimu Imperial Expansion: The First Phase

Chimor, however, wholly unlike its Inca successors, was slow to initiate long-range conquest, and it was not until about AD 1130, several centuries after the birth of Chan Chan, that a more ambitious stage of imperial conquest can be identified by archaeologists, as opposed to mere local expansion. North-west of Chan Chan there is evidence of battles fought at about that date in the Río Jequetepeque Valley at Talimbo. Chimor also at this time took control of Pacatnamu, an important ceremonial centre located at the point where this river reaches the coast; however, the great site of Farfan, situated at some distance inland, has now come to be viewed as the probable centre of Chimu power in that region. The ruins of Farfan (its earliest radiocarbon date is AD 1155 ±130) is the biggest site in the Río Jequetepeque Valley and contains six spacious rectangular compounds, of which certain details relate to the *ciudadelas* of Chan Chan itself. The largest of these bears a certain resemblance to the Uhle compound at Chan Chan. Its burial platform was used only once for a high-status individual. As we shall later see, the Spanish chronicler Calancha in 1638 wrote an account of the Chimu conquest of the Jequetepeque region by a General Pacatnamu that can perhaps be related to these more recent archaeological finds. Very little space at Farfan appears to consist of domestic quarters and the evidence indicates that it was a major administrative centre, used for the political control of the surrounding region. The limited size of storerooms in Farfan suggests that they served for luxury goods rather than for standard agricultural produce.

Much less is known about any corresponding Chimu conquests southwards from Chan Chan in this first major stage of expansion. Carol J. Mackey suggests that they did not extend beyond the Río Santa Valley, some 200 kilometres south of Chan Chan and where, as mentioned above, Cerro Coronado was situated. During this period it

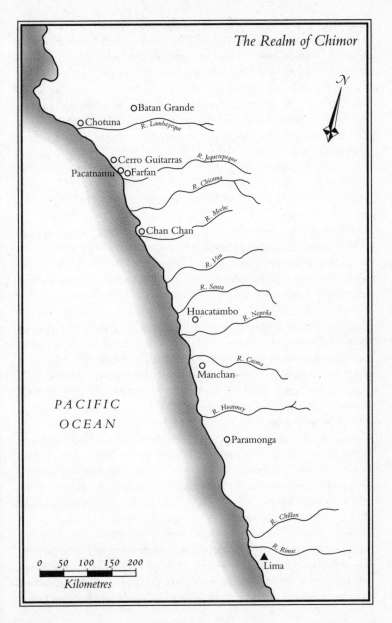

The Realm of Chimor

N

Batan Grande

Chotuna

R. Lambayeque

Cerro Guitarras

R. Jequetepeque

Pacatnamu Farfan

R. Chicama

R. Moche

Chan Chan

R. Viru

R. Santa

Huacatambo

R. Nepeña

R. Casma

Manchan

R. Huarmey

PACIFIC
OCEAN

Paramonga

R. Chillon

R. Rimac

Lima

0   50   100   150   200

Kilometres

seems that Chimor also extended its hegemony inland from the capital somewhat further up the Río Moche Valley to the vicinity of the modern town of Poroto. This advance appears to have been a costly process, to judge by the many vestiges of Chimu fortifications which they were apparently forced to build, as the price of establishing closer contacts with the more productive sierra. Poroto offers good access into such territory in the form of routes that could lead foot and llama caravans from an elevation of 700 metres to lands situated at 3400 metres above sea level.

Further Conquests

The time interval between the establishment of Chan Chan and the era of its first phase of more extensive conquest was, as we have already seen, somewhat prolonged. Its domain both to the south and to the north only reached its fullest extent after conquests were made some four to five hundred years after the foundation of the capital.

Following the first phase of major conquests described above, the best evidence of a second stage of expansion, at least a century later than the Río Santa Valley invasion, derives from the Río Casma Valley. In the large site of El Purgatorio, a form of pottery was produced known as Casma incised. Certain Chimu remains have also been found at El Purgatorio, though much of this site was then apparently abandoned, since the invaders preferred to construct their own principal centre of power at Manchan; they also built two other centres near the Río Casma mouth. In addition, the Chimu occupied no fewer than ten other administrative sites and five villages in the Río Casma Valley. (The settlements defined as administrative are those which contain adobe or stone compounds divided into rooms and courts.)

The principal site of this region, Manchan, is vastly greater than all others in the valley, covering an area of sixty-three hectares. Most of the inhabitants lived in cane-walled structures, which yield evidence of the production of copper artefacts and textiles; one of these structures was a specialized copper workshop. The relatively late establishment of Manchan has been confirmed in recent years; seventeen radiocarbon samples ranged between AD 1305 and 1430. Carol Mackey and Ulana

Klimyshyn tentatively associate both these dates and the characteristics of local Chimu ware found in Manchan with the Velarde *ciudadela*, the sixth of the ten palace compounds of Chan Chan, generally dated to between 1300 and 1350. Direct comparisons between Chan Chan and Manchan, however, are hard to draw; the presence of first-level administrators is not in evidence at Manchan, while those of the second and third levels, like their counterparts in Chan Chan itself, were not interred in burial platforms; they built modest storage facilities, as compared with those of the palaces of Chan Chan.

Yet further to the south, beyond the Río Casma Valley, the evidence suggests that Chimu control was never consolidated to the same degree as in the northern reaches of their empire. Only in the Río Casma Valley and that of the Río Nepeña a little further to the north, does evidence exist of a full degree of imperial control. Chimu pottery has been found as far south as the Huaura Valley, but as yet no Chimu centres of power. Ethnohistorical sources, however, suggest that Chimor influence extended further southwards through the Chancay Valley and even as far as the Río Chillon, lying just to the north of Lima, where vestiges of Chimu pottery and other artefacts have been found. The striking Chancay ceramic style, with fine vessels charac-terized by black on red painting on a white slip, was common to both valleys before any Chimu incursion occurred. Chancay motifs are usually geometric but plants, animals and people were also depicted. Chancay tombs contained seated figures clad in elaborate textiles.

Lambayeque

The second stage of the Chimu conquest northwards beyond Farfan is dated by Christopher Donnan as beginning in about 1370 and is thus more or less contemporaneous with the second southward advance to the Río Casma Valley. In this northward expansion Chimor now faced the well-established and widely diffused Lambayeque culture. This culture was first thus named by Larco-Hoyle in the 1940s, based on the term used by Cabello de Balboa in his sixteenth-century account of the myth and history of the region. The term Sican (the indigenous name of the important site of Batan Grande) has also been used for the same culture. Lambayeque crafts are often confused with the better-known Chimu objects. But while both cultures owed much to Moche traditions, Lambayeque pieces are often aesthetically superior, though some of them, such as the beaten gold masks, are apt to be attributed to the Chimu.

Between 1980 and 1982 Donnan excavated the almost contiguous sites of Chotuna and Chornancap, lying about sixteen kilometres to the south-west of the town of Lambayeque. Chotuna, until then not even accurately mapped, consists of a series of palaces, pyramids and walled enclosures scattered over an area of about twenty hectares; of these only a fraction is still visible today. The walls of one such pyramid are covered with friezes that probably belong to the middle phase of the site, thus predating the Chimu occupation. Chornancap, on the other hand, consists of a single truncated pyramid, adjoined on its north side by an extensive area of adobe structures, complete with rooms, corridors and open courtyards. The chronology of Chotuna can be divided into three approximate phases, the first from AD 700 to 1100, the second from 1100 to the Chimu occupation in about 1370, and the third from 1370 to 1600, embracing the Inca conquest of about 1470 and the subsequent arrival of the Spaniards. The Chotuna friezes bear a remarkable similarity to those of Dragón, in the Río Moche Valley adjacent to Chan Chan, though they differ in certain details. In both places the predominant theme is a double-headed serpent that does not figure in Chimu imperial iconography.

Donnan's account is partly concerned with a possible relationship between Chotuna and the local Naylamp dynasty of Lambayeque, described by the historical sources. A distinct difference in style marks the transition from the first to the second Chotuna phase, occurring in about AD 1100, and possibly caused by severe flooding. In recent years there has been copious evidence of the devastating havoc wreaked by that rare catastrophe called El Niño. In a normal year no rain falls near the coast; however, torrential rainfall and destructive floods may occur as a result of this phenomenon which was capable of bringing about radical changes, even involving the irrigation systems on which the people of the coastal desert depended. Donnan confesses that it is not altogether clear whether the notable changes of about AD 1100, perhaps attributable to the El Niño phenomenon, marked the beginning or the end of the legendary Naylamp dynasty of Lambayeque, described in Spanish sources and discussed in more detail below.

Izumi Shimada, in dealing with another important site, Batan Grande, situated in the Lambayeque Valley more than one hundred kilometres from Chotuna, prefers to use the term Sican rather than Lambayeque to define its successive periods. As in the case of Donnan's dating, only the last of the three phases marks the Chimu occupation. Early Sican begins in about AD 700, following the demise of the Río Moche Valley hegemony of the region; middle Sican dates from around AD 900 to 1100, while late Sican ends with the Chimor intrusion, tentatively set at some time after 1350. Batan Grande, notable for the size and number of its buildings, tends to be regarded as the main administrative centre of the Lambayeque Valley. Though apparently unfortified, Batan Grande occupies an enormous area; it contains major pyramids within its precinct, together with cemeteries and elite residences, stone quarries and copper mines; areas cultivated with irrigation canals have also been identified. Studies of Batan Grande have located literally thousands of important graves and much of the surviving Peruvian gold objects were taken from this vast burial site, of which a single tomb is known to have yielded over 200 gold and silver necklaces, together with countless artefacts decorated with jewels.

Shimada's chronological periods are somewhat differently defined from those of Donnan. Whereas Donnan's first phase at Chotuna continues until about AD 1100, Shimada describes a marked change in about AD 900, when his mid-Sican phase begins. Middle Sican iconography is distinguished by the presence in art forms of an almost ubiquitous figure described as the Sican Lord. This lord, the hallmark of middle Sican iconography, has been tentatively identified by Shimada as Naylamp, founder of the legendary Lambayeque dynasty, thus implying his arrival in about AD 900, rather than in either AD 700 *or* AD 1100, as proposed in Donnan's account. The Great Sican Lord is often described as a 'bird man', since he is frequently displayed with small wings, beak-like hooked nose and talon-like feet. On certain vessels he appears as if in flight, mounted on a serpent with a head at each extremity of his body. The head of the Sican Lord was often modelled on the spout of vessels flanked by two serpent heads, a common Moche motif. Hence middle Sican ceramics, usually burnished black and

Figure 22 The Sican Lord Mounted on Serpent

brown wares, often depicting the Sican Lord, form a style that is readily recognizable, and very different from that of Chimor itself.

In contrast, late Sican vessels are marked by an almost total absence of the Sican Lord, and are largely devoid of what might be described as ideological motifs.

The Northern Frontier

Finally, in defining the ultimate limits of Chimu expansion, (reported in historical sources to have extended as far as Tumbez on the Ecuadorian border), the far north coast of Peru also needs to be considered; it is separated from Lambayeque by the Sechura Desert.

The mountainous but arid coast is dissected by three river valleys, the Piura, Chira and Tumbez. This region between the Sechura Desert and the Ecuadorian border is a zone of transition between the intensely arid Peruvian coast and the tropical landscape of Ecuador. The upper Río Piura Valley lies partly within the rainfall zone and has the largest irrigated area of any coastal Peruvian valley. The Chira, further to the north, is the third largest Peruvian river in terms of water discharge. Pre-Inca ceramics found in the Piura region are as follows: Phase I, AD 500 to 700; Phase II, AD 700 to 1000; and Phase III, 1000 to 1450. Only in the second part of Phase III is an imperial Chimor presence reflected in ceramic styles.

There are seventy-eight recorded sites in the upper Río Piura Valley. Perhaps the more markedly Chimu is Chalacala in the upper Río Chira Valley, a site dominated by a series of walled compounds and a large rectangular enclosure. There is, moreover, a striking similarity between adobes at Pacatnamu, on the Río Jequetepeque, and the circular adobes of the Río Piura and Chira Valleys.

None the less, ceramics truly indicative of either Sican or Chimu influence are rarely present in the surface collections from the Río Piura and Chira Valleys and from available data we do not know whether this area was truly conquered or simply subjected to certain Chimu influences. The region was perhaps a crucial link in the maritime trade between Ecuador and Peru, involving above all the highly prized spondylus shells from the north.

The Imperial City

Among the most puzzling aspects of the realm of Chimor are those related to Chan Chan itself. Though it was the capital of a major kingdom, it becomes hard to describe as a city, in the accepted sense of the word, a place that is devoid of squares and streets. The real unit is not the city but the compound, or *ciudadela*, each with its almost Cyclopean surrounding wall, whose proportions seem to exceed any security threat. Chan Chan is thus unique and its layout wholly distinct from that of other known centres.

The site is large, measuring about twenty square kilometres, about a third of which forms the urban nucleus. The maximum population has been estimated at 36,000. Radiocarbon dates are few and inconsistent; in general terms an absolute chronology of AD 900 to 1200 may be proposed for early Chimu, 1200 to 1300 for a middle phase, and for late Chimu 1300 to 1470, the approximate date of Inca conquest.

Depending on whether the earliest constructions are included, there are at Chan Chan nine to eleven majestic compounds. (The term 'palace' may be less appropriate since certain doubts exist as to how far each one may be attributed to one or more rulers.) The whole of the interior walls seems to have been decorated with huge adobe friezes which impressed earlier explorers. The walls in the Velarde group, discovered in 1980 but destroyed by torrential rains a few years later, were among the most imposing.

As described by Alan Kolata, the first two compounds were built in the south-east sector in about AD 900. The city then expanded to the north with the construction of two compounds named after the German archaeologist Max Uhle, and then subsequently to the west, where a further two compounds arose. The northern extremity was completed by the erection of the largest of all, called the Gran Chimu; the city thereafter grew back upon itself and the last enclosures were built near the coast. The compounds vary greatly in size, ranging from 72,000 square metres to a maximum of 265,000 square metres.

In the central sector of each compound is the focal point – the great burial platform – apart from the Laberinto compound, which inexplicably has no platform. The second important feature of each compound consists of the structures known as *audiencias*, whose function is generally thought to be administrative. Initially the *audiencias* were constructed within the compound, but during middle Chimu times, they began to be placed in the annexes of each enclosure. The *audiencias* are usually so small that they could comfortably hold only one seated person. Frequently the walls were adorned with adobe friezes. Apart from the central tomb and the *audiencia*, the compounds contained wells and storage space, as well as other rooms, whose small size is more suggestive of marketing activities rather than of use for habitation. The greater nobles are thought to have lived and worked in the elaborate northern annexes of the later compounds, as opposed to the central platform, the private area where royalty held court. Smaller enclosures also adjacent to the compounds are interpreted as possible residences of minor nobility and state functionaries, while a third type of construction, rather prosaically described as Siar (small irregular agglutinated rooms), seemingly housed most of the urban population, many of whom were craftsmen. Storage facilities were found mainly inside or adjacent to the compounds.

Figure 23 Portion of Chan Chan Palace Frieze

The exact significance of each compound has been subject to several interpretations; no artefacts have been found that might help to clarify the issue. The archaeological data tend to support the attribution of each compound to a single ruler (the number of compounds and of rulers mentioned in the ethnohistorical accounts tend to correspond). According to this assumption, an individual monarch, whose burial platform formed the central sector of the structure, bequeathed his estate to a kind of guild, consisting mainly of relatives or descendants, and the compound then became an institution, perhaps comparable to the imposing establishments of deceased Inca monarchs that were maintained in perpetuity and were known as *panacas*. This practice is generally described as 'split inheritance', whereby each former monarch's estate was preserved separately.

The Chroniclers' Version

At this point it becomes appropriate to consider the surviving fragments of the story of Chimor as related by Spanish chroniclers. As we shall see, they are rather cryptic, as compared with the copious data provided in recent decades by archaeological research both on the site of Chan Chan and on its expansion to the south and more particularly to the north.

In general terms, leading archaeologists, far from rejecting the chroniclers' story as sheer myth, have sought to reconcile the ethnohistorical data with their own findings.

John Rowe, in summarizing these documents in 1948, suggested that much additional material on the history of Chimor still remains undiscovered in Peruvian and Spanish archives; such hopes have not as yet been altogether fulfilled.

The principal surviving document is the 'Anonymous History of Trujillo', of which the first chapter contains a brief summary of the history of Chimor. This chapter was first published by Father Rubén Vargas Ugarte in 1936, taken from a manuscript found in Lima; the beginning is incomplete, due to the damaged condition of the document. As summarized by Rowe, the story is as follows. A man named Taycanamo, or Tacaynamo, came to Chan Chan on a log raft; he was dressed in a cotton breechcloth; he brought with him certain magic yellow powders. He did not relate whence he came, but declared that he had been sent by a great lord from across the sea for the purpose of governing Chimor. During the first year he built a shrine, where he performed certain rites using his yellow powders. Having been acclaimed as ruler by the local inhabitants, he learned their language and became known as 'King of Chimor'.

Taycanamo's son, Guacricaur, made only limited conquests, and it was his son and heir, Nancen-pinco, who really laid the foundations of the kingdom, not only by expanding his realm inland as far as the head of the Valley of Chimor, but by conquering part of the coast, advancing northwards towards the Río Zaña and south as far as the Río Santa, thereby acquiring a kingdom which stretched for about 200 kilometres from north to south. Seven rulers succeeded Nancen-pinco and made further conquests, but the 'Anonymous History' only names the last of these rulers, Minchancaman, who reigned at the time of the Inca conquest by Tupac Inca in about AD 1470.

An account of dynastic details related to the northern Río Lambayeque Valley, later absorbed by Chimor, is provided by the important chronicler Cabello de Balboa, who himself resided in 1581 in Lambayeque. According to Cabello, the first historical ruler, Naylamp, came from the far south on a fleet of rafts with his wife, Ceterni, together with a harem and a group of court attendants; he bore a green stone idol named Yampallec. (Cabello states that the name Lambayeque was derived from Yampallec.) Naylamp ruled for many years, after he had first established a settlement and built a great palace at Chot. He had numerous children; he was secretly buried by his attendants, who then proclaimed throughout his realm that he had taken wings and flown away. His eldest son, Cium, inherited his kingdom and ruled for many years.

Nine named rulers in turn succeeded Cium, of whom the last was called Fempellec. He decided to move the great idol of Yampallec from Chot. After several abortive attempts to do this, the devil appeared to him in the guise of a beautiful woman. He slept with her and immediately rains began to fall of an intensity unknown in this desert kingdom. Disastrous floods followed; to punish Fempellec for the suffering inflicted upon his people, they took him prisoner, tied his feet and hands and threw him into the sea. With his death the lineage of the native lords of Lambayeque ended and the kingdom was conquered by the king of Chimor, who installed as his subject ruler a lord called Pongmassa; his grandson, Oxa, was ruling in his place at the time when the Inca conquest occurred.

It should be added that, according to the chronicler Antonio de la Calancha, who wrote in 1638, Jequetepeque, lying to the south of Lambayeque, had been previously conquered and annexed by a Chimu military leader called Pacatnamu. The king of Chimor rewarded him by naming him as governor of the Río Jequetepeque Valley, which the general ruled from a capital called by his own name, Pacatnamu.

Scholars have endeavoured to relate these rather cryptic accounts of the deeds of these legendary dynasties of Chan Chan and Lambayeque to the archaeological research of recent decades. As Michael Moseley points out, while Taycanamo is named as the founder of the Chan Chan dynasty, we are told very little as to his achievements. He is a rather elusive figure; he founds no monuments and performs no heroic deeds. Given the future power and prestige enjoyed by Chimor, this unembellished account of its antecedents seems paradoxical. Moreover, little is told of his heir, Guacricaur, who reportedly made modest advances inland. Perhaps more characteristic of the role of a true founder is the third ruler, Nancen-pinco, who enlarged his kingdom by making more spectacular conquests, the extent of which the 'Anonymous History' perhaps exaggerated; such achievements might, in fact, have spanned several generations.

Archaeological evidence, as we have seen, places the conquest of Jequetepeque at around AD 1200, but dates the founding of Chan Chan to nearer AD 900. Hence the 'Anonymous History' has to be regarded as a most incomplete document, in that the first three centuries of Chimu history are seemingly compressed into the reigns of only three kings. Following a long series of anonymous rulers after Nancen-pinco, Minchancaman is a much more concrete figure, who allegedly ruled all the coast from Tumbez to Carabayllo, just north of Lima, at the time of the conquest by the Incas, who carried him off to Cuzco. Assuming that the full subjection of Lambayeque can now be correctly dated to the second half of the fourteenth century, it thus precedes the Inca conquest of Chimor by scarcely a century and should therefore be attributed not to Minchancaman, but to his more immediate predecessors.

Christopher Donnan, in writing of Chotuna, describes that site as presenting a chronological sequence that is reasonably comparable with the Cabello account of the Naylamp dynasty. As we have seen, he first tentatively dates the early phase of Chotuna from approximately AD 750 to 1100 and points out that in recent years substantial evidence has emerged of the occurrence of a major El Niño flood that had a dramatic effect; it seems even to have caused the abandonment of Pacatnamu, situated about eighty kilometres south of Chotuna, while there is also evidence of major flooding in the Río Moche Valley at this time, as well as of other disasters in the region.

Donnan offers two possible chronologies for the dynasty of Naylamp and his ten named successors, assuming that they indeed existed. The

first, as explained above, relates Naylamp with the foundation of Chotuna in about AD 750, and his last successor, Fempellec, with a catastrophic situation created by the El Niño flood at the end of the eleventh
century AD. Alternatively, he suggests that Naylamp's arrival could also
correspond with the period *following* this devastation and his dynasty
could then be correlated with a later phase of Chotuna, which dates
from approximately AD 1100 to AD 1300. On the one hand, it was
during this phase that were painted the great friezes associated with a
double-headed serpent, which might bear some relation to the traditions
of the Naylamp dynasty. On the other hand, there is no evidence of a
major El Niño at the end of this period.

Hence it becomes impossible on the one hand to date the Naylamp
dynasty with any certainty; none the less, archaeological research in no
way demonstrates that the story is purely mythical; an event such as
the thirty-day rain mentioned in the Cabello narrative is by no means
impossible for the northern coast of Peru. Moreover, the excavation
of Chotuna could equally have demonstrated that the Naylamp story
did *not* correspond to the site, either if it had been built, say, in AD
500 or, alternatively, if it had been demonstrably a late construction,
corresponding more with the Inca occupation of the region.

Other suggestions have been made which diverge from Donnan's
two alternative solutions and which date Naylamp more on the basis
of art forms than of natural catastrophes. As we have seen, Izumi
Shimada suggests a possible identification of Naylamp with what he
calls the Great Sican Lord, the ubiquitous anthropomorphic figure
who assumes a dominant position in middle Sican art, centred in the
Lambayeque region, but disappears abruptly in the late Sican period.
Shimada thus relates the legend of the arrival of Naylamp neither with
early Chotuna of the eighth century nor with the phase of Chotuna
that begins in the eleventh century, but more with the period of the
Great Sican Lord, which dates from about AD 900, and is closely
associated with the site of Batan Grande. Middle Sican ended not with
a flood but with a widespread fire that destroyed several of the principal
sites.

Chimor: Arts, Crafts and Commerce

Chimor's greatest artistic achievement surely lies in the field of architecture. Outstanding in this respect is the great Chan Chan itself and its spectacular monuments, described above. Chan Chan was, moreover, a city of craftsmen, noted above all for its metalware; copper, bronze, gold and silver were all used; gold and silver were hammered into fine goblets, together with many masks, plates and earplugs. A major proportion of the surviving pre-Hispanic gold objects of Peru derives from the Chimor period. Apart from gold and silver, much use was made of bronze, widely employed after about AD 1000 to make ornaments, weapons and tools, both hammered and cast. Much of what is described as Chimu art in fact originated in Lambayeque. Many of the well-known beaten gold masks were also made by Lambayeque craftsmen, though after this region had been conquered by Chimor, some of these metalsmiths were transferred to the capital of Chan Chan. Chimor is

Figure 24 Chimu Painted Earspool

Figure 25 Chimu Blackware Vessels

also distinguished for its pottery, of which so much has survived, in particular the characteristic blackware, though much red pottery was also produced.

Many types of ceramics, in particular the stirrup-spout vessels, recall Moche designs, including the double-spout jars; Chimor figures tend to be rather stylized and few could be described as portrait jars of the kind made in Moche times. Most vessels were made in moulds and the pottery was mainly mass-produced and thus tends to be less stylistically creative than that of the Moche. Musical instruments are an important motif in which the central figure often plays a drum. Some Chimu textiles are well preserved, including tapestries. Plain cloth was also decorated by painting, while fabricated pieces include breechcloths, headbands or turbans, together with large mantles.

Chimu artists were highly valued by the Incas. Many were taken off to Cuzco, where they enjoyed great prestige; in contrast, very little Inca pottery is to be found in the Chimor region.

In general terms, while some Moche forms survived, many basic themes of Chimu art mark a major departure from the more standard Moche style. The site of Galindo, with its large enclosure some forty kilometres inland from Chan Chan, has been described as a Moche antecedent for the earlier Chimu *ciudadelas*. However, Galindo corresponds to Moche V, which, as we have seen, differs greatly from Moche

IV, involving a change of stylistic emphasis, in the form of a shift towards maritime themes, seldom present in earlier Moche ceramics. Characteristic of Moche V art, as a precursor of Chimu, is the presence of various sea gods, together with the distinctive theme of boats made of rushes, often figuring two men in rush boats; one of these wears a short shirt and bears war-clubs and shields, while the other boatman, with a long shirt and an elaborate head-dress, is surrounded by rays. Also characteristic of Moche V is the anthropomorphized wave, in which a paddling boatman deity struggles in a fight against a fanged supernatural figure. An almost identical anthropomorphized wave is to be found in a frieze in the Uhle enclosure in Chan Chan, which is one of the earliest structures, thus presenting a continuity between Moche V and Chimu art themes.

In general, marine iconography is predominant in Chimu art, and was present in many of the friezes that adorned the ten great enclosures of Chan Chan; other friezes illustrate birds and various animals. The maritime shift that began in the Moche V period and which reached its culmination in Chimu art illustrates the increased importance of the sea, and in particular of maritime trade, in the economy of the region. Typical of this new emphasis are the rafts, bearing warlike maritime deities, that carry cargo and sometimes even prisoners. Whereas the ocean was previously shown as the scene of ritual fishing, it now assumes a new importance related to maritime commerce. Such art does not specifically depict those seaborne dynastic founders, Naylamp and Taycanamo, but indirectly implies that their stories are related to oceanic travel.

While other forms of maritime trade probably increased in importance in Chimor times, the specifically religious significance of at least part of the cargo stresses the predominant role of the spondylus shells in Chimu ritual. *Spondylus princeps* is native to Ecuador and is not found in the colder waters of the Peruvian littoral. Spondylus does not figure in traditional Moche art, though another form of conch shell occurs in the late Moche V phase. Thus, while spondylus shells were less often depicted during the Early and Middle Horizon, the situation changed dramatically with the florescence of Chimor.

The Chimu elite used the shells in unprecedented quantities and at Chan Chan royal burials were accompanied by stupendous offerings of shells, whole, cut and pulverized as dust. Imposing caches of spondylus have also been found at El Dragon in the Río Moche Valley. The management of the great spondylus trade may have originated in the principality of Lambayeque. Thirteen examples of Lambayeque and of middle Sican art (*circa* AD 900 to 1100) illustrate divers collecting spondylus shells. In one mass burial from the middle Sican period, no fewer than 400 spondylus shells were found, interred with an estimated 200 humans who had been sacrificed. Illustrations survive of diving techniques to catch the spondylus and even of the rafts used to transport the treasured shells. On a textile in San Diego's Museum of Man, the motif in each case is a raft depicted as a straight bar topped by what is either a sunshade or a mast, and which carries two people on deck. These divers hold implements that may have been used to pry the shellfish away from the rocks to which they were attached. Various middle Sican earspools show a curious spondylus diving motif; they illustrate a boat, apparently made from balsa logs, that seats two individuals who hold lines attached to two other individuals in the water below the boat with a small object attached to their belts, perhaps a diving weight. Other metal earspools carried a much simplified version of shell diving, in which a single central figure seems to replace the boat and its two occupants.

Such illustrations found in Sican art have no counterpart in Río Moche Valley Chimu, nor in southern Ecuador itself, but since spondylus procurement has an ancient history in Ecuador, it seems likely that the divers portrayed in such objects were Ecuadorian. We know that much of the coast of Ecuador was then controlled by the kingdom of Salangone, a polity whose principal source of revenue was maritime commerce. Bartolomé Ruiz, pilot of the conquistador Francisco Pizarro, spotted a raft, presumably of the type used in this trade, which was laden with goods, including what are identifiably spondylus shells. Illustrations of balsa rafts used in the centuries after the Conquest correspond to the craft illustrated in Sican art; the shape of most of these is flat and blunt-nosed; the raft seen by Ruiz even possessed a cabin.

It may be added that the Great Sican Lord is sometimes illustrated as bearing a spondylus shell, a detail that has led to suggestions that a characteristic figure such as Naylamp might conceivably have played a leading role in the popularization of the *Spondylus princeps* as an item of deep religious significance, attaining the status of a treasure to be associated with royal burials.

While maritime trade and imported goods thus seem to have played a more important part in its economy than in that of its Inca conquerors, Chimor was also notable for the copious output of the work of its local craftsmen, not only in terms of quantity, but also, as we have already seen, of quality. As a result of major excavations carried out in the 1970s, it became clear that the main occupation of the population of Chan Chan was craft production on a large scale; such research suggested the presence of many full-time specialists, probably organized in hierarchical guilds.

Such craft production seems to have developed at a fairly late stage in the history of the kingdom. Much of our knowledge of large-scale weaving of fine cloth and elaborate metalworking derives from the last century before the Inca conquest. During this pre-Inca effloresence the surviving evidence suggests that the bulk of the common people lived in four *barrios*, or districts, that housed some 25,000 persons, of whom nearly half were craft specialists. Within each *barrio* the artisans were housed in single family units. Such units, excavated in the *barrio* adjacent to the *ciudadela* Laberinto, contained family kitchens, together with storage space. Most houses seem to have served both for metalworking and for the production of fairly elaborate textiles. While there is evidence of woodwork and the fashioning of stone objects, the main emphasis was on metallurgical production, of which so many examples survive.

Hence it may be logical to assume that Chan Chan, while it imported certain luxury items, as depicted on frescoes of seagoing rafts, also enjoyed a substantial export trade, based on high-volume production of certain items.

What is not absolutely clear is whether its artisans traded their own goods with the urban population and with other centres controlled by Chan Chan, or whether such trade was confined to a specialized merchant class. However, to judge by the apparent volume of production, it would appear that this exceeded what was needed solely for the city itself. Such merchants, assuming that they existed, would have also imported essential raw materials, such as alpaca wool for fine textiles, as well as metal ingots, probably from the mineral deposits situated inland, at the headwaters of the Río Moche, and such exchange networks

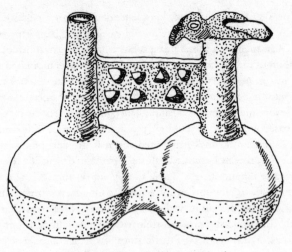

Figure 26 Chimu Double-spout Vessel

probably extended not only along the coast but inland into the highlands and perhaps beyond.

What is evident from such research is the degree of concentration of craft production in Chan Chan itself. For instance, excavations in the important administrative centre of Farfan, as well as of other sites to the north of the Río Moche Valley, reveal little evidence of such activities on a comparable scale in such places. If such crafts were practised in the provinces, the output was more limited. Equally, storage facilities located in Chan Chan itself are vastly greater than those located in provincial centres.

The Chimu State

It finally remains to consider in general terms the nature of the Chimu state, the basis of its economy, and in particular the extent to which it may offer a precedent to the achievements of its Inca conquerors. At the time of the Inca conquest, the Chimu monarch, like his Inca counterpart, was by definition a divine ruler. Certain doubts may persist as to whether the king had enjoyed such an elevated status since earlier times, or, alternatively, that this was a later development, perhaps dating from the conquest of Lambayeque. However, the basic structure of Chan Chan suggests a hierarchical society, with the royal tombs as the focal point of each of the vast palace enclosures; the grandiose northern enclosures moreover suggest the presence of an elite class of nobles, whose importance increased as part of the process of imperial expansion.

The economy of the early Chimu state (AD 900 to 1100) was probably more based on local agricultural production, though following the forceful military expansion initiated towards the end of this period, Chimor conceivably began to be more dependent on outside resources.

The early Chan Chan was able to depend on the resources of the nearby coastland, reinforced by a process of sunken garden farming involving the use of shallow wells. The first phase of expansion led to the control of the upper reaches of the Río Moche and to the development of canal systems protected by fortifications. Evidence also exists of the presence of coastal settlers in later periods in the highlands, reaching as far as the Cajamarca region; their presence was probably due to the need to control canals to feed the hydraulic systems of the growing coastal population.

The quest for increased agricultural resources was also a likely motive for the continued coastal expansion, particularly southwards to the Río Casma Valley, where Manchan and other Chimu administrative centres are concentrated in areas endowed with much arable land, the control of which was surely one of the main functions of Chimu administrators in this valley. The concentration of settlements on the Río Casma, which has a dependable water flow, suggests that the control of this water was an important consideration. In the Río Chicama and Jequetepeque Valleys to the north of Chan Chan, administrative centres (with the notable exception of the apparent provincial capital, Farfan), are located where they could best control irrigation canals and surviving evidence suggests that El Niño of about AD 1100 did much damage to this irrigation system. It should be added that by late Chimu times, say from AD 1300, possibly due to devastation caused by earlier El Niño flooding, the Chimu made only limited attempts to maintain and restore their local irrigation systems; following the annexation of Lambayeque a trend is evident of greater reliance on revenue derived from new resources acquired by their expansion, a view that is reinforced by the increased size and structure of storage space in the imperial capital.

In considering Chimu expansion, the importance of the eventual absorption of Lambayeque becomes clear. Lambayeque was a formidable polity and contains more large ruins than any other Andean area, and many of its massive monuments are related to the Chimu culture. The occupation of the rich and powerful northern kingdoms during the later phases of pre-Inca Chimor is thus a crucial factor. None the less, it would seem that in both the northern and southern extremities of their realm, the Chimu tended to leave much power in the hands of local lords; Chimu domination does not seem to have been very disruptive of previous economic patterns, unlike the more far-reaching effects of Inca rule, as we shall later see.

It appears that particularly with respect to its southward expansion, Chimor preferred to share power with the traditional rulers. Archaeological research in the Río Casma Valley suggests that the Chimu showed little tendency to change existing forms of government.

In this southern region, in the four administrative centres that were studied, only two have compounds built by the invaders. In the architecture at Manchan, the principal centre, local and Chimu styles are blended and evidence for the respect for the powers of the local lords suggests the continuance of existing patterns of rule. However, in the northern reaches of their empire, Chimu influence on architecture seems to have been greater than in the south. For instance, in Farfan, one compound contains a burial platform that recalls those of the great enclosures of Chan Chan itself.

The surviving evidence suggests that Chimor's phase of major military expansion belongs mainly to the final centuries of its existence as a major state (radiocarbon dates for Chimu occupation of the Río Casma Valley, lying less than halfway to its ultimate southern boundary have now been recalibrated to give an average figure of about AD 1300). Even after such expansive policies had been adopted, while the local lords retained a certain authority and while use was made of the local hierarchy for administrative purposes, overriding policy dictated that power should continue to be concentrated in Chan Chan. In a physical sense, this principle is confirmed by the vastly greater size of Chan Chan itself as compared with any provincial centre.

Such disparity, as already stressed, is confirmed by the great disparity between the amount of storage facilities available in the capital and in other centres. In two provincial centres that have been fully excavated, such research has failed to reveal large numbers of storerooms. In Farfan about half the storerooms lie behind the main burial platforms, suggesting that they were designed to contain elite types of goods rather than comestibles. The comparison of Inca and Chimu storage facilities suggests a basic difference between the two systems. Chimor storage capacity appears to have relied more heavily on craft production, while the Inca pattern allowed for much larger volumes of staple goods.

Certain evidence suggests that the power and influence of a class of nobles of the highest rank were enhanced during the culminating phase of long-range conquest; such predominance was based on the notion of divine kingship which had surely become a predominant feature of Chimor at the time of the Inca conquest.

Possibly the concept of a divine ruler was not a feature of the original structure of Chimor, but developed gradually. In the later palace enclosures the central part became an increasingly private space, which was almost certainly reserved for the king and his principal attendants. Equally striking is the gradual development of more elaborate northern annexes to the palaces, perhaps the residences of high-ranking nobles, who came to form an elite class of administrators. At the same time the notable expansion of storage space occurred, more probably devoted to the accumulation of luxury goods, marking the transition to an extractive tribute economy. A comparison with the architecture of provincial centres such as Manchan suggests that such top-level administrators were not present in regional centres. On the contrary, as we have seen, the evidence points to a certain Chimu reliance on sharing power with an existing local elite, while resettlement of population was kept to a minimum.

The question as to how far a divine or semi-divine Chimu ruler shared power with an associate, as so often occurred in Peru, remains a somewhat open question, though Patricia Netherly tends to insist that on the north coast no ruler governed alone. As she remarks, while European chroniclers were intent upon offering king-lists of ancient dynasties, Andean accounts are more concerned with an attempt to define, or redefine, the social order, and persons or events closer to the present outrank those further away. Hence, for instance, the story of the Naylamp dynasty and its disastrous ending under Fempellec is, as we have seen, hard to firmly associate with any known series of events, including the El Niño phenomenon, which occurred more than once. Given the Andean proclivity to record more recent names and events, it might be more realistic to associate Naylamp and his successors with the period that followed rather than with that which preceded the great El Niño of about AD 1100.

The Chimu ruler, Minchancaman, is easier to place since he is named as the king who succumbed to the Incas in about AD 1470. He was carried off to Cuzco and married to a daughter of the Inca. When the Incas abducted this last ruler, unquestionably Chimor under Inca rule continued to be an elitist society in which high-ranking lords mobilized human energy to serve the conquerors, though the Incas eliminated the top level of Chimu administrators. The chronicler Augustín de Zarate relates that a rebellion occurred against Inca occupation, and that thereafter the coastal peoples were not allowed to bear arms. As a result of the uprising many more people from Chimor were removed from their homeland and taken to Cuzco. Hence, while Chimu power was obliterated, aspects of their art and culture survived and, as we shall later see, the Inca monarchy itself displays certain features that may have already prevailed over the course of many centuries in the van-quished coastal kingdom.

CHAPTER SIX

THE RISE OF THE INCAS

The last pre-Hispanic era in the history of the Central Andes is that of the Inca Empire. Initially a small tribe of uncertain origins that had settled in the Valley of Cuzco, their conquests dwarfed those of earlier Andean peoples and are more comparable in their extent to those of the great empires of the Old World.

In the period between the fall of Huari and the rise of the Inca, from about AD 1000 to 1400, while the kingdom of Chimor dominated the north coast, smaller maritime principalities flourished further to the south. Conspicuous among these was Ychma, situated astride the Lima Valley. Remains of its principal city, Cajamarquilla, still survive in a suburb of present-day Lima. Yet further to the south, the Ica and Nazca peoples continued to weave fine textiles and produce distinctive forms of pottery.

In highland Peru, however, a certain power vacuum seems to have existed in the post-Huari era. For instance, the Valley of Cuzco itself was inhabited by peoples who lived in hilltop settlements and produced a pottery known as Killke. Fairly recent excavations tell us that Pikillacta, the great Huari site situated within the Valley of Cuzco, was abandoned long before the Inca era.

Due to the absence of any writing system and to a paucity of post-Conquest texts in their native Quechua, much of our knowledge of the Inca past stems from Spanish conquistadors and chroniclers.

Their reports initially had little impact on the non-Spanish world. It was not long, however, before the Incas began to attract a wider audience. Descriptions of a veritable mountain of silver discovered by the Spaniards at Potosí, in the Bolivian *altiplano*, enriched the legend of a remote and mysterious El Dorado, famed for its riches. Soon dramatic stories of the Spanish absorption of the Inca realm and of the tenacious native resistance began to spread, and written reports began to circulate in Italy and France, replete with tales of Peruvian wealth, exemplified by the huge ransom of pure gold offered to the conqueror Pizarro by the fallen emperor Atahualpa. As early as 1534, a broadsheet was printed at Lyon entitled 'Nouvelles certaines des isles du Pérou'. In the seventeenth century writers such as Locke in England and Spinoza in Holland began to extol the primitive realms of the American Indians and in particular those of Peru.

The notion of the noble savage, applied originally more to the natives of Brazil, took firm hold of the imagination of the French eighteenth-century philosophers, stimulated by reports of a great kingdom centred upon the High Andes and endowed with fabulous riches. Voltaire chose Lima as the setting of his *Alzire*, an extremely successful play. His most famous work, *Candide*, published in 1759, offered an idealized account of an El Dorado whose denizens were supposedly descended from the Incas. The work of Jean-François Marmontel, *Les Incas ou la destruction de Pérou*, dedicated to King Gustav III of Sweden, was published in 1777. The action, mainly concerned with the fate of Atahualpa (aided by refugees from the fallen kingdom of the Aztec Moctezuma), takes place in Quito.

In marked contrast to such exotic tales, William Prescott in the 1840s published his *Conquest of Peru*. Using Spanish sources already published, he related in his stately prose the epic of the conquest of Peru, beginning with the bizarre story of the Spaniards' first meeting with the Inca Atahualpa.

In the early twentieth century, Peru began to attract an increasing number of authors of a different kind. No longer romanticized as greedy and gaudy capitalists, solely obsessed with the hoarding of gold, the Incas were now more often portrayed as the world's first socialists, and at times even described as communists!

More recently the Incas and their predecessors have been the subject of intensive study by scholars of many lands, whose work has produced spectacular results, even if much still remains to be done.

Humble Origins

In contrast to the more grandiloquent accounts of their triumphs and tragedies, the story of the humble origins of the Incas is more diffuse. The Spanish chroniclers generally concur in naming as their creator god Tici Viracocha, a deity linked in legend with the shores of Lake Titicaca. Among the most vivid descriptions of Inca origins is that of Juán de Betanzos. He relates that the creator, Tici Viracocha, at a time when all was still dark, ruled over certain people whose name no one recalls. The god then emerged from Lake Titicaca, killed these shadowy beings who had somehow offended him and turned them into stone. Arising once more from the lake, he created the sun and moon, and thereafter fashioned new beings, some of whom were pregnant women; these he dispatched to different destinations, including Cuzco.

While Viracocha is the more usual appellation, the Inca creator is sometimes associated with Pachacamac (meaning 'world creator' in Quechua), who was the patron deity of the famed coastal shrine of that name. However, the locus for the act of creation is essentially Lake Titicaca; among the Aymara peoples of that region, their thunder god, Thunapa, was also worshipped as a primordial deity.

In Andean cosmogony, there is little emphasis on the creation of the world *ex nihilo*, as related, for instance, in the Book of Genesis. Chroniclers prefer to write of tutelary gods who proceeded to create humankind in a world that already existed, though often described as lacking sun and moon, a feature reminiscent of Mexican legends, already known to the Spaniards. In one such Andean version the first beings are turned into black cats, in another into monkeys; only subsequently was the human race created, including, of course, the Incas.

Hence surviving Spanish accounts deal less with the primordial creation of man on another continent than with events when humans already lived in the Andean region, an omission that is hardly surprising; for Spanish chroniclers, imbued with the marvel of God's creation of the world as described in their own scriptures, it would have been a blatant heresy to accept any notion of a second creation in the New World, complete with its own Adam and Eve, living in an Andean version of the Garden of Eden.

Thus it needs to be stressed that we have a dual cycle of origin myths, one of which centres upon Lake Titicaca and the ancient site of Tiahuanaco, and is based upon the creation – in fact a second creation – of the sun and moon, and stresses the role of the creator Viracocha. But in addition to such myths, what amounts to an alternative version tells how the first Inca ruler, Manco Capac, emerged from Lake Titicaca and thence travelled literally underground to the cave of Pacariqtambo in the Valley of Cuzco. In view of the sanctity of ancient fables related to the shores of Lake Titicaca in pre-Inca times, any links with such traditions gave added legitimacy to Inca claims to conquer other peoples. Somewhat paradoxically, the identity of Pacariqtambo, a focal point of the Inca myths associated with the Valley of Cuzco, is far from clear, since Gary Urton has demonstrated that the present-day town of that name did not come into existence until 1571.

Moreover, the true date of the appearance of the Incas in the Valley of Cuzco remains uncertain. Following excavations in 1994 and 1995 at Chokepukio, twenty-seven kilometres south-east of Cuzco, Gordon McEwan views the pre-Inca culture of Killke as ending in about AD 1200 and treats the site as Inca rather than pre-Inca from AD 1200 onwards.

While scientific evidence may thus advance the possibility of an earlier Inca presence, chroniclers offer a fairly uniform version of the appearance of this exiguous band of Incas in the Valley of Cuzco at an implicitly later date. Their story can be summarized as follows: when they emerged eventually from the cave of Pacariqtambo to the south-east of Cuzco, their leader, Manco, was accompanied by three brothers, each with his sister–wife. As they proceeded on their way, one brother, Ayar Cachi, was induced to enter a cave to retrieve some golden cups. A godlike figure of prodigious strength, he could cast stones that would level whole hills. But after Cachi entered the cave his brothers proceeded to bar the entrance. Thus trapped, he was turned to stone and his *huaca* became one of the most holy objects in Inca ritual. (The countless sacred stones, known as *huacas*, scattered throughout the Inca realm, played a major role in their cosmogony, as we shall later see.) After Manco and his band had reached Huanacauri, a hill some thirteen kilometres from Cuzco, a second brother, Ayar Uchu, was also transformed into a stone *huaca*. The third brother, Ayar Auca, reportedly then grew wings and was ordered to take flight and to proceed ahead of Manco to Cuzco; when he alighted there he became the community stone called Cuzco Huaca, the field guardian of the city.

Having disposed of his brothers, Manco, unchallenged by rivals, proceeded to Cuzco accompanied by his sister—wife and by those of his three brothers. Accounts imply that the site was already occupied and describe hostile encounters between Incas and peoples known as Huallas and Alcavizas; the small band of Incas held their ground and established themselves in the triangle between the Tullumayo and Huatanay rivers, where Manco reportedly built the first Coricancha temple.

The Early Rulers

Having outlined what are in effect legendary accounts of the foundation of Cuzco, in this chapter a summary follows of what we learn from the chroniclers of Inca history, prior to the arrival of the Spaniards. The two following chapters are devoted to other aspects of the brief, if spectacular, period of Inca achievement, such as their cities, including Cuzco, their lifestyle, and above all their system of control over the huge empire which they conquered.

The chroniclers mainly concur as to the names of the first seven Inca kings, listed as follows by John Rowe:

Manco Capac
Sinchi Roca
Lloque Yupanqui
Mayta Capac
Capac Yupanqui
Inca Roca
Yahuar Huaca

A few writers, such as Garcilasco de la Vega, credit these rather nebulous early rulers with spectacular conquests; according to this chronicler, the third king, Lloque Yupanqui, had already advanced into the province of Collao, situated on the shores of Lake Titicaca, while the fourth, Mayta Capac, occupied the ancient site of Tiahuanaco and thereafter subdued the Arequipa region. Earlier twentieth-century writers on Inca history, such as Clements Markham, tended to accept this version of events; Philip Ainsworth Means, whose *Ancient Civilizations of the Andes* was published in 1931, not only treated as fully historical the orthodox list of early rulers, but stretched their chronology, crediting them with the conquest of the Lake Titicaca region in about AD 1200.

It might be added that while certain scholars now tend to the view that the Incas arrived in the Valley of Cuzco much earlier than the chroniclers' accounts might imply, they do not suggest that at such a stage they made far-reaching conquests.

Notwithstanding a few reports of spectacular triumphs, most accounts are vague and contradictory to a point that it becomes hard to offer a historical version of this early Inca period reign by reign. Of Manco's successor, Sinchi Roca, almost nothing of note is recorded, while the third ruler, Lloque Yupanqui, is generally portrayed as pacific or inactive. The fourth king, Mayta Capac, reportedly clashed with the Alcavizas, described as 'natives of Cuzco', thereby implying that the Incas were not the first to occupy that place and that their hold was as yet partial and tenuous. This tribe allegedly assaulted the Incas when Mayta Capac's father still reigned and reached the walls of Coricancha, their sacred stronghold.

Several accounts offer a confused tale of how the Alcavizas dispatched 'ten Indians' with the intention of killing Mayta Capac and his father, Lloque Yupanqui, who was still king at the time, in their abode in Coricancha. Pedro Sarmiento de Gamboa relates that the prince, Mayta Capac, killed one of the ten Indians by hurling a ball with which he was playing at the time; the others immediately fled. Thereafter a magic hailstorm, more devastating than Mayta's well-aimed missile, put the Alcavizas to flight. The prince soon ascended the throne, but apparently then ruled peacefully and fought no more wars.

The sixth ruler, Inca Roca, is generally named as the first to divide Cuzco into Hanan (upper) and Hurin (lower) Cuzco. Henceforth, the rulers no longer lived in the temple enclosure of Coricancha, situated in Hurin, but each built his palace in Hanan Cuzco. The division of Andean cities into upper and lower halves, which still persists in certain instances today, became widespread in Inca times, if not before, and occurred in places as distant from one another as Puno on Lake Titicaca, the Cañari region of Ecuador, and the ancient cities of the south coast of Peru. Even the Chancas, who, as we shall see, were to become the Incas' implacable foes, were divided into Hurin and Hanan Chanca, each with its own ruler; as also became the case in Cuzco, Hanan was the more dominant of the two. In the Inca capital, while the rulers who succeeded Inca Roca built their palaces in Hanan, Hurin none the less retained a certain prestige as the residence of the religious hierarchy, based upon Coricancha.

Among the inveterate foes of the early Inca rulers was another group, the Ayarmacas, against whom many chroniclers write of warlike encounters with the Incas during the reign of Inca Roca. Foremost among these is the report of the abduction by the Ayarmacas of Roca's son and heir, Yahuar Huaca; sequestered when only a child, he was forced by his captors to serve as a simple herdsman for a whole year. Then after a hard-fought battle, the prince was rescued and the rift between Incas and Ayarmacas was, at least temporarily, healed by a double marriage between their ruling houses.

John Rowe, who may be regarded as the pioneer of modern Peruvian ethnohistory, poses the question as to whether the seven rulers who preceded the eighth, Viracocha Inca, made any real conquests. He concludes that the supposed triumphs of these kings were probably little more than raids and that the same localities tended to be repeatedly lost and regained in successive reigns. However, Rowe opines that none the less, even if their hold on the surrounding region was tenuous, the first seven Inca rulers named in the texts may have achieved at least a certain primacy over their nearest neighbours, though not the capacity to exact regular tribute.

At first sight one may be tempted to agree with scholars who dismiss the rather nebulous story of these seven monarchs as mere fiction. But in the final instance, if these monarchs were expunged from the record as pure figures of fable, then one has to replace them with anonymous leaders, and to credit the latter with more or less the same achievements, namely the feat of securing over the course of a few generations a certain degree of control over the Valley of Cuzco, as a prelude to the spectacular achievements of their successors. The seven early rulers might perhaps be compared with the Albany king-list which, by a most curious coincidence, also consists of seven shadowy monarchs who ruled before Rome became a conquest state, whose existence it may now be fashionable to deny, and whose principal function, whether legendary or historical, was to bridge the gap between the fall of Troy and the foundation of Rome.

Myth and History

Given the nebulous nature of accounts of the early kings, the obvious question then arises as to the sources available for the study of the more dynamic period of Inca expansion that followed. In the absence of any body of pre-Hispanic documents, or of post-Conquest accounts written in the native Quechua, attempts to provide a history of the Inca rise to power present inevitable problems and many doubts remain unresolved. As we have seen, sixteenth- and seventeenth-century writing on the Incas was mainly the preserve of chroniclers, writing in Spanish, in contrast to Mexico, where pre-Hispanic pictorial codices survive, as well as copious documentation in the Nahuatl language provided by informants soon after the Conquest. Most of our data – with the exception of the illustrated text of Huaman Poma de Ayala, whose copious illustrations with written descriptions of the Incas and their conquerors are unique in their detailed portrayal of those involved – thus derive from purely Spanish sources; while the opinions of their authors may differ, they tend to describe Inca society from a European viewpoint.

These chroniclers gleaned their data from oral traditions passed from one Inca generation to another. Much of their information derives from the elite of Cuzco and therefore reflects more the state system of the capital than the situation of the empire as a whole. Lacking written texts that predate the arrival of the Spaniards in Peru, it becomes hard to judge how far events recorded in the chronicles are truly historical; accounts of the acts of Inca kings may at times merely represent purely Spanish interpretations of the Inca hierarchy, based on European notions of kingship and in particular on European principles of dynastic succession.

The Incas, while they had no writing system in the accepted sense of the word, did have an excellent method of recording certain data, the *quipu* knotted cords that served as an elaborate method of keeping records. The *quipu* was a single cord to which were attached strings, some of which ran parallel, while others sprang from a common starting point. By means of knots and distinctive colours the strings could express both numbers and meaning. Paradoxically, however, few if any of the copious *quipu* data seem to have reached the Spanish chroniclers, though the latter at times refer to the *quipocamayos*, the highly skilled specialists who managed the *quipu* system.

Existing *quipus*, taken mainly from cemeteries, cannot today be related to the objects with which they were buried. These surviving *quipus*, found mainly in the desert regions of the coast, separated from persons and artefacts after their removal from graves, were dispatched individually or in mixed bundles to different museums; hence the work of an individual *quipocamayo* becomes impossible to identify. We do know that the *quipus* served to compile such vital statistics as crop yields and storage capacity, as well as to record data on manpower, basic to military planning. Following the Spanish Conquest, *quipus* were still used to compile data on the damage done to crops and homes in places where Spanish forces had passed.

Had the demand arisen, the *quipu* system could surely have served admirably to record other information, such as the precise length of each ruler's reign. Unfortunately, however, the Incas' interest in their dynastic chronology seems to have been minimal. Hence *quipus* offer no information on such matters. The Spaniards who actually took part in the Conquest form a unique category of information; as eyewitnesses, they offer vivid portrayals of Inca life and ritual of which, however, they understood little. For instance, one may cite the riveting account by Francisco de Xerez of the first meeting between Atahualpa and his captor, Francisco Pizarro; Xerez even gives a detailed description of the ruler's house in Cajamarca. He also wrote of the great temple of Pachacamac which he visited when it still functioned as a centre of pilgrimage.

One major problem for modern scholars is the fact that the two most detailed and systematic accounts of Inca history, those of Sarmiento de Gamboa and of Cabello de Balboa, were both written many decades after the Conquest, at a time when few eyewitness informants were still alive. As we shall later see in more detail, their versions, while

Figure 27 The Ruler's Chief Accountant, Holding Quipu
(illustration by Huaman Poma)

differing in certain respects, draw much information from one or more common sources. Sarmiento's history was commissioned by the Viceroy, Francisco de Toledo, and completed in 1572. His work, based on meticulous research, was none the less somewhat biased against the Incas, since Toledo aimed to establish that the Incas were mere usurpers rather than rightful owners of the vast domain that they ruled at the time of the Conquest. Much of Cabello's narrative, written in 1586, clearly follows that of Sarmiento, while describing in more vivid detail the protracted and savage Inca wars against the tribes of Ecuador, where Cabello himself had lived.

In contrast to these chroniclers, the *Comentarios Reales* of Garcilasco de la Vega, published in Lisbon in 1609, offer a vigorous apologia of Inca conquest. The author himself was of Inca lineage; though he quotes earlier chroniclers verbatim, his portrayal of his Inca forebears as kindly despots presiding over a vast welfare state, acquired with a minimum display of force, tends to be treated nowadays with some circumspection. Nearly half a century later, in 1663, Father Bernabé Cobo wrote his *Historia del Nuevo Mundo*. Using all the sources then available, his cogent and valuable appraisal is more that of an historian rather than a chronicler.

A much earlier and somewhat more pragmatic portrayal of the Inca achievement is given by Cieza de Léon. His viewpoint is generally pro-Inca without, like Garcilasco, attempting to idealize their rule. Cieza first travelled through Colombia and Ecuador before arriving in 1548 in Peru; his account offers information supplied mainly by the Inca nobility. Among such earlier chroniclers, Juán de Betanzos, who married a daughter of Atahualpa and who spoke fluent Quechua, was well placed to record the Inca version of their own traditions.

While the work of a few such authors was published relatively early, many others lay buried for centuries. The *Señorío de los Incas* of Cieza de León was first printed in 1880; Sarmiento's history, finely bound, was sent to King Philip II; the manuscript eventually reached the library of the University of Göttingen in 1785, but remained unpublished until 1906! Part of the work of Betanzos was already known, but his full text was first discovered in the 1980s in Mallorca and published in 1987 in Madrid.

Certain other chroniclers merit special attention. Polo de Ondegardo, a distinguished jurist, offers valuable information on social matters; he wrote in the 1560s and 1570s. He is much cited by Bernabé Cobo. In fairly recent times, our knowledge of the Andean past has been enriched by the publication of a whole series of *Visitas* made by Spanish adminis-trative inspectors to imperial provinces; prominent among them is the

Visita of Garci Díez de San Miguel made in 1567 to the Aymara province of Chucuito, and the 1562 *Visita* of Iñigo Ortiz de Zuñiga to Huánuco.

Pachacutec

Viracocha, the eighth ruler, and his heir, Pachacutec, may at least claim to be historical figures, in contrast to the seven earlier kings mentioned above, whom some treat as authentic rulers while for others they belong more to the realm of fiction.

Leading chroniclers, such as Sarmiento, attribute to this eighth ruler, Viracocha, the conquest, or reconquest, of places near Cuzco that had been reportedly taken by former rulers and later abandoned after they had rebelled. According to such writers, Viracocha not only consolidated Inca control of Cuzco itself, but made more distant conquests than his predecessors.

But accounts of Viracocha's achievements are at times so nebulous as to prompt leading scholars, such as María Rostworowski, to question whether he existed at all, and to suggest that Viracocha and his heir, Pachacutec, might have been one and the same person. Even assuming that Viracocha was indeed an historical personage, his reign is often described in terms that savour of legend as much as fact.

Garcilasco de la Vega in particular offers a wholly different version of events, insisting that it was Viracocha rather than his son Pachacutec who fought and defeated the Chancas, a triumph which, as we shall see, was the turning point in Inca history. According to Garcilasco, Viracocha, having crushed the Chancas, launched ambitious campaigns and conquered a vast realm. In other words, many of the more spectacular achievements of Pachacutec are merely transposed backwards in time by this author and attributed to his father.

Many chroniclers concur in describing Pachacutec as Viracocha's legitimate son and heir, and hence as the ninth ruler. Certain accounts, however, confuse the issue by stating that Urco, an illegitimate son of Viracocha, was this ruler's personal choice as successor; Cieza de León even states that Urco actually reigned for a short time before being deposed by Pachacutec and then murdered.

The Chanca threat had apparently already arisen before Pachacutec's accession; so little is known of them that one can only speculate as to their origins. At all events, in the more standard versions of the story, they had in the earlier part of Viracocha's reign occupied the region of Andahuaylas, lying to the west of the Valley of Cuzco, a feat which brought them to within striking distance of Inca-dominated territory.

The Chancas did not, however, penetrate the Valley of Cuzco itself until Viracocha was already an old man. At this stage, however, fear of these intruders provoked such terror that many Incas abandoned all hope of resistance. Among these was the aged Viracocha, who fled from Cuzco accompanied by Urco, his heir, and took refuge in a fortress situated at some distance from the capital.

The more standard version of the events that followed may be summarized as follows. Pachacutec, backed by two able generals and a staunch band of nobles, stood firm, resolved to defend Cuzco to the last ditch. The Chancas invested and tried to storm the city. In various accounts, Pachacutec is alternatively portrayed as human conqueror and legendary hero. In one such version, at this crucial juncture the tide of fortune turned dramatically as the very stones were transformed into armed warriors at Pachacutec's behest. Thus reinforced, the attack was repulsed; the stones were thereafter collected and placed in the principal shrines of the city. In further encounters Chanca forces were crushed and retreated from Cuzco towards Andahuaylas. The two leading Chanca generals were killed; their heads were displayed on lances and their skulls were made into drinking cups. Pachacutec bore the insignia of the defeated Chancas to his father, Viracocha; according to most accounts, Viracocha then abdicated and Pachacutec ascended the throne as the tenth Inca monarch.

Following the Chanca rout, Pachacutec assumed supreme control. According to the principal sources, his reign marked the transformation of the early township into a resplendent capital, the reordering of the priestly hierarchy, and the moulding of primordial cults into a dynamic force, the spiritual expression of the Inca will to conquer.

The rebuilding in Hurin Cuzco of the great shrine, formerly also the residence of the ruler, was the first task. Coricancha was an imposing enclosure in which the largest building was the Temple of the Sun. Today walls and broken rooms of the complex survive, forming the shell of the Dominican monastery, though none of the walls existing

Figure 28 Pachacutec Inca (illustration by Huaman Poma)

in the Dominican cloisters today can be identified as proven relics of
the Sun Temple.

Flanking the Sun Temple were other sacred buildings, housing gods,
priests and *mamaconas*, the countless temple women, later brought to
Cuzco from all quarters of the empire and schooled in fine weaving,
in the making of *chicha*, the ritual drink, and in many other sacred tasks.

Under his successors Coricancha was continually embellished, but
Pachacutec gave the Temple of the Sun a special aura by placing therein
golden statues of the former rulers, splendidly attired and fully armed.
A new image of the sun god, Inti, was cast in pure gold; before this

idol llamas and priceless vestments were burned in sacrifice, while numerous children, both boys and girls, were buried alive in front of the image. The chronicler Juán de Betanzos relates that Pachacutec also adorned the Sun Temple with a second golden statue, the image of a boy, who recalled a figure that had miraculously appeared to him on the night before his triumph over the Chancas. When the king prayed before the statue, it reportedly spoke to him. Only the greatest nobles were allowed to venerate this image.

Apart from temples, the city was now adorned with imposing palaces, including that of Pachacutec himself. Though its exact location is hard to identify, one palace, called Casana, is attributed by some to Pachacutec, but is more generally known as that of his grandson, Huayna Capac.

Pachacutec totally revamped the structure of Sacsahuaman, the great fortress that dominated Cuzco; its dimensions are, however, so vast as to suggest that its completion was the work of several generations of rulers. The edifice served as the city's main storehouse for arms and clothing, as well as for massive quantities of jewels, gold and silver later paid in tribute.

Pachacutec did not confine himself to rebuilding the city and renovating its infrastructure; his impact on the social fabric of the community was profound. The original Incas, often kinsmen of the ruler, were called *orejones*, thus named because their ears were pierced with large holes. They were divided into eleven *ayllus*, best described as kin groups with descent in the male line.

A major problem, however, arose because these original Incas, or *orejones*, belonging to the eleven *ayllus* linked by blood ties, were too few in number to meet all the needs of an expanding state. To remedy the situation, Pachacutec relied on an additional class, 'Incas by privilege', (*por privilegio*), who formed another ten *ayllus* that also became part of the Cuzco establishment. The title 'Inca by privilege' was gradually extended to include many of those who spoke Quechua, drawn from the surrounding region.

Pachacutec established a corvée system to provide labour needed for the erection of an imperial capital. Of this an essential element was the use of *mitimaes*, a procedure that reached major proportions as the empire was expanded; *mitimaes* consisted of large groups of people, arbitrarily transplanted from regions already subdued, and settled in newly occupied lands in order to further their adaptation to Inca rule; in return, people from certain regions were settled in the Valley of Cuzco. As we shall later see in more detail, the *mitima* system was basic to the Inca method of imperial control.

The strange custom prevailed in Cuzco whereby the descendants of deceased monarchs formed a group known as a *panaca*, whose mission was to conserve the dead ruler's mummy and to immortalize his achievements. The *panacas* might have existed earlier in Inca history, perhaps inherited from Chimor, but Pachacutec consolidated the system. He reportedly disinterred the bodies of the first seven rulers and fashioned mortuary bundles of their remains, that were then set on thrones in the Temple of the Sun beside his own father.

Pachacutec's first long-range conquests imply the existence of at least an embryo version of the Inca road system, later to attain such spectacular proportions. It is possible that roads served military purposes in the Huari period, but the Inca system enjoyed a unique symbolism of its own, with its four principal roads radiating from the centre of Cuzco, dividing both the capital and Tahuantinsuyu, as the empire came to be called, into four quarters: Chinchasuyu, Antisuyu, Collasuyu and Cuntisuyu (often written as Condesuyu in the sources).

Early Conquests

The Inca victory over the Chancas served as a springboard for an explosive territorial expansion, though the gains made by Pachacutec himself as opposed to those of his successors are not easy to define. His first task was to complete the conquest – or reconquest – of the Valley of Cuzco and the surrounding region, in which the Incas were now the paramount power.

Following this process of consolidation, accounts survive of an expedition to Collao, led by Pachacutec in person, in which he encountered the peoples of the Lake Titicaca region. After a hard-fought battle he took the important centre of Hatunqolla; the defeated Colla ruler was sent to Cuzco and subsequently beheaded. The Lupaqa Indians, whose capital city was Chucuito, reportedly then also surrendered;

thereafter Pachacutec visited the great ruins of Tiahuanaco; amazed by the fine stonework, he took careful note of the methods of construction, with a view to his own rebuilding of Cuzco.

The last major campaign of Pachacutec's reign was directed north-west towards Huánuco and led to conquests in the mountainous interior of present-day Peru. The general who commanded this expedition was Capac Yupanqui, Pachacutec's brother; however, he advanced beyond Huánuco and occupied Cajamarca. In doing so he had far exceeded his instructions and, notwithstanding his triumphs, was executed on return to the capital.

By all accounts Pachacutec enjoyed a fairly long reign, during the latter part of which one of his sons, Amaru, subsequently replaced by Tupac Yupanqui, served as co-ruler. John Rowe, on the basis of a chronology offered by Cabello de Balboa, suggests that he reigned from 1438 to 1471, but Rowe acknowledges that such dates are tentative, since no proven Inca dating system exists.

Pachacutec may, according to certain reports, have survived as co-ruler during the first part of the reign of his successor, Tupac, but after the expedition to Cajamarca he in effect fades from the scene and both the reins of government and the military command were assumed by Tupac.

Since Pachacutec presents a dual aspect, as legendary creator and human king, it becomes hard to separate the two and to assess his historical role. If he laid the foundations of a state ordained to rule a boundless empire, some doubts linger as to how far all its institutions really owe their origin to this one ruler. Certain scholars may prefer to stress his semi-divine nature as creator more than conqueror, as the successor to Manco, the original founding father. But while it may be perfectly legitimate to question the traditional accounts of such prodigious achievements, much evidence does suggest that in an historical sense his reign initiated the expansion of Tahuantinsuyu. When he became ruler, the Incas formed only a modest village community. By the time of his death they already controlled an expansionist empire.

The Last Emperors

Tupac Yupanqui, the ninth Inca, while not, like his father, Pachacutec, venerated as a cultural hero, was none the less a genial commander. In Inca tradition his martial skills were legendary; at his death the Incas ruled a vast domain, stretching for over 3000 kilometres from northern Ecuador to central Chile; in terms of sheer distance this feat bears comparison with the triumphs of Alexander the Great, whose furthest penetration into Asia, achieved with the decisive aid of horses and chariots, brought him to the River Oxus, a distance of some 4000 kilometres as the crow flies from his home base in Macedon.

The chroniclers Sarmiento and Cabello de Balboa give a fairly detailed and in many respects parallel account of the conquests of Tupac and his successor; the much earlier work of Cieza de León, and the later version of Cobo, in very general terms offer similar data.

According to both Sarmiento and Cabello, in Tupac's first campaign he took the northward road to Chinchasuyu, occupied Cajamarca and pressed on to the north-west, reaching as far as Tumebamba (the present-day Cuenca) in Ecuador, the home of the Cañari people, who still occupy the surrounding country. Tumebamba became the northern capital of the empire, a second Cuzco, the remains of whose temples and palaces so impressed Cieza on his journey through Ecuador, though few vestiges survive today. Tupac reportedly also conquered the Quito region but, as we shall see, neither chroniclers nor archaeologists accept the notion that Quito ever became the principal Inca centre in that region.

The four Spanish sources mentioned above concur that Tupac then descended from Tumebamba to the Ecuadorian coast and, proceeding via Tumbez, undertook the conquest of Chimor, a major feat of which only the very briefest accounts survive. The ruler was carried off to Cuzco and the great kingdom was annexed. Following the assault on Chimor, Tupac visited the great shrine of Pachacamac; this was more a ceremonial visit than a conquest, involving a consultation with the famous oracle. The emperor then established control over many ancient principalities situated on the southern coast of Peru, such as Ica and Chincha. At first sight the notion that such kingdoms should surrender their freedom almost without a fight might surprise. However, due to

Figure 29 Topa Inca in His Storehouse in Collao (illustration by Huaman Poma)

the ability of the Incas to form large armies by recruiting subject peoples and hence to achieve a crushing superiority in numbers, resistance in some cases already seemed futile. In addition, in desert regions on the coast the invaders could deal the defenders a deadly blow and even force surrender by cutting off the intakes of the irrigation canals on which they depended for their food supply.

This great series of conquests, reportedly ranging from central Ecuador to southern Peru, was followed by an expedition embracing an even vaster extent of territories, but of which only the most fragmentary accounts survive. Tupac marched south-eastwards to Lake Titicaca. He overcame some resistance in Collao, and then forged on and took the important centre of Cochabamba, also situated in Bolivia. After a further advance into what is now north-western Argentina, his campaign ended in Chile where, according to most accounts, the Río Maule, to the south of the present-day capital, Santiago, formed the southernmost limit of Inca conquest.

While ethnohistorical material on Inca penetration of north-west Argentina is almost non-existent, local sources, such as Gerónimo de Bibar, describe the fierce resistance offered by the peoples of Chile, led by two principal chiefs, Michimalongo and Antalongo. These sources suggest that in Chile the Inca invaders finally encountered an almost total rejection and had to fight fierce battles to achieve their conquests.

But quite apart from cryptic records of such a spectacular series of conquests, in contrast more copious accounts survive of the rather fruitless but endless struggles by Tupac and his successor against primitive peoples who lived to the east and south-east of Cuzco on the hot and humid slopes of the Andes, as they descend eastwards towards Amazonia. While somewhat hollow victories are invariably reported, these campaigns seem to have achieved relatively little, and in a climate so inhospitable to the Incas that they suffered serious losses. As an example may be cited Sarmiento's report of how in one of these arduous forays beyond the Andean peaks, 'Among the most terrible and fearsome mountains with many rivers', many soldiers died of sickness; Tupac with the survivors, only a third of the original force, wandered lost in the mountains for many days until rescued by Achachi, a leading Inca commander. The chronicler duly explains that Peru is cool and dry, whereas the *montañas* (i.e. the eastern slopes of the Andes) are warm and humid.

Tupac thereafter returned to Cuzco where he built and adorned great palaces and fortresses. Exhausted by endless intrigues, he fell sick and would see no more visitors. When about to die, he summoned the nobles, his relatives, and told them that he was about to depart for the house of his father, the sun.

The Inca Empire in 1532

Pasto

COLOMBIA

Otavalo
Quito
Lacatunga

R. Santiago

ECUADOR

Guayaquil
Tumebamba

Tumbez

R. Marañón

Ayahuaca
Huancabamba

BRAZIL

Lambayeque
Cajamarca
Chan Chan
Huamachuco

R. Huallaga

Huanuco

Bonbon
Xauxa

PERU

Pachacamac — Lima

Huari

Vilcabamba
Machu Picchu
Ollantaytambo
Cuzco

Chincha
Pisco

Huamanga

BOLIVIA

Ica
Nazca

Puno
Arequipa ▲
Chucuito
Copacabana

Lake Titicaca

▲ La Paz
Tiahuanaco
Cochabamba ○ Incallacta

Arica

Porco ○ ▲ Potosí

PACIFIC
OCEAN

CHILE

Cachi

Tucuman

Copiapo
Pucara de Andagala

○ Inca town

━━ Approximate limits of
the Inca Empire

▲ Modern city

━·━·━ Modern political boundary

Coquimbo

ARGENTINA

0   200   400   600

Kilometres

▲ Mendoza
▲ Santiago

R. Maule

N

Pachacutec, following his defeat of the formidable Chancas, is generally accepted as the ruler who transformed what was at best a city-state into an expanding empire by means of long-range military expeditions.

But Tupac was clearly a genial commander who, according to all surviving accounts, conquered an immense territory stretching from Ecuador to central Chile. The obvious question then arises: how, faced with the formidable difficulties of conducting campaigns at such distances from their home base, did they vanquish and subdue vast numbers of different peoples so remote from Cuzco? These peoples were fighting for the freedom of their homesteads; they faced no such problems of logistics as beset the Incas and endured no gruelling marches to reach the field of battle. But against such opposition, while the Incas reportedly suffered many setbacks, they ultimately prevailed.

Moreover, while the Incas profited from their superb lines of communication, scarce evidence exists that they were better armed than their adversaries; their weapons did not constitute any advance over those of other Andean peoples, and certainly did not impress the Spaniards, who marvelled at their roads and buildings. While the sling was also one of their principal weapons, a favourite arm was the club, originally fashioned from stone but later made of hard jungle palm with a head of bronze, a weapon that can still be seen in many museums and collections. Such clubs were hardly effective against the Spaniards, since they had to be lifted above the head to inflict a blow, whereas the Spaniards could dispatch Indian after Indian with lightning sword thrusts. In effect, the Inca armament scarcely presents a very major advance on that of the Moche rulers, whose warriors, depicted on their pottery, also used large clubs a thousand years earlier, together with slings and spear throwers.

Nor can Inca triumphs be easily attributed to superior tactics. They perhaps had the advantage of being nearly always on the offensive against opponents who adopted a rather passive defence and appear to have taken few steps to cut the Incas' seemingly vulnerable lines of communication. But while it might be conceded that the Incas, as the attacking force, held the initiative, the chroniclers' reports, particularly those of Cabello de Balboa on the hard-fought Ecuadorian campaigns, suggest that both sides adopted almost identical tactics, often based on a strategy of fortified strong points and aggressive sorties.

Inca success might perhaps be attributed more to the skill and determination of their high command. The rulers were served by generals of unquestioned skill; in many instances such commanders were close relatives, brothers or sons and nephews of the king.

But sound leadership, let alone weapons or tactics, hardly explain the Incas' dazzling record of victory. Their triumphs are perhaps better explained by their skill in deploying superior numbers at the crucial point by drawing on the manpower of an expanding domain. If the Incas suffered a setback, say in Ecuador, they could use their road and message network to quickly summon reserves of Collas and others who were firmly loyal to the empire, while their opponents, worn down by a tide of fresh levies, could not themselves replenish their strength, depleted by the first battles. Hence Inca conquest might be attributed, at least in part, to their political skill in indoctrinating former foes, now subject peoples, who were by then willing to trek immense distances and risk their own lives for the sake of their previous conquerors.

Huayna Capac

As often occurred, the succession was disputed; a plot was hatched, fomented by female intrigues, to supplant Tupac's chosen heir with another son whom the ruler had formerly proposed as his successor. With the backing of Tupac's brother, the plot was foiled and his designated heir, Huayna Capac, duly mounted the throne.

Huayna Capac was still a young man when he became ruler. Having first performed the elaborate funerary rites for his father, he headed for the north on his first campaign. Certain descriptions of his route and objectives on this and other expeditions bear an almost uncanny resemblance to those followed by Tupac. But it must always be borne in mind that our information derives from verbal traditions based on individual memories, leading to possible confusions between one reign and another in the reports of Spanish chroniclers who recorded those traditions. Archaeology at present tells us more of the ultimate extent of such conquests than of the order in which they occurred.

After Huayna Capac's first brief expedition to Cajamarca and beyond,

1. *Ritual chamber, Galgada*

2. *Main temple, Chavin de Huantar*

3. *Panoramic view of main temple, Chavin de Huantar*

4. *Moche pottery figurine vessel*

5. *Moche pottery bird-shaped vessel*

6. *Moche pottery portrait vessel*

7. *Moche pottery house vessel*

8. (Right) Moche pottery stirrup-spout vessel

9. (Below) Nazca bridge-spouted pot

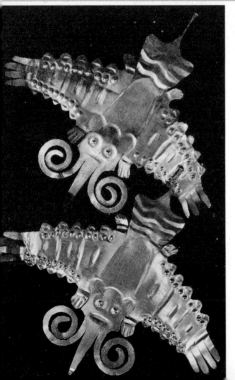

10. (Above) Nazca painted bowl with turkey vulture motif

11. (Left) Nazca objects, hammered gold, perhaps representing humming-bird-moths

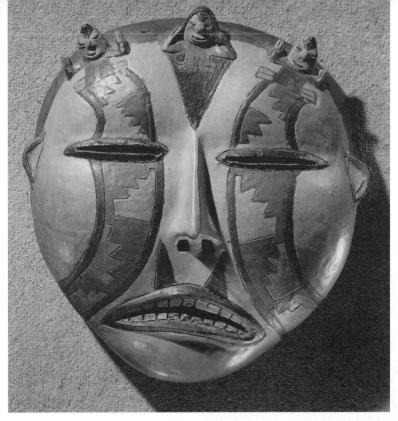

12. *Paracas pottery mask*

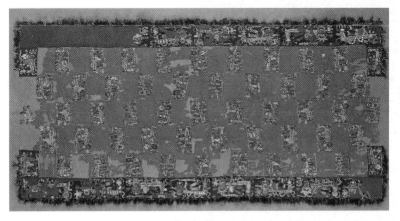

13. *Large embroidered Paracas mantle*

14. *(Above) Tiahuanaco: stairs to the Kalasaya temple, beyond which stands the monolith*

15. *(Left) The monolith: a richly attired figure holding a beaker and a short sceptre*

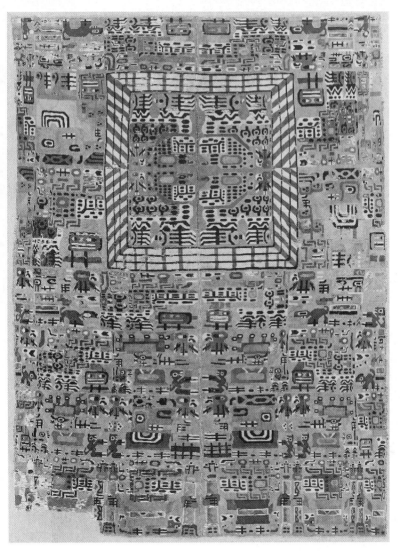

16. Poncho, late coastal Tiahuanaco

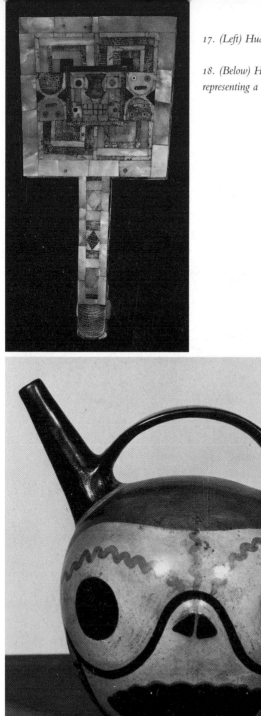

17. *(Left) Huari mirror*

18. *(Below) Huari double-spout bottle representing a skull*

19. *Chimu ceramic bottle*

20. *Chimu tapestry poncho*

21. (Above) Chimu disc in hammered silver

22. (Left) Chancay mantle with bird motifs

23. Inca poncho

24. *Inca silver figurine*

25. *Inca fortress at Sacsahuaman*

26. *The twelve-sided stone*

27. The church of Santo Domingo in Cuzco built on the mortarless stones of the Coricancha

28. Statue of Francisco Pizarro in his birthplace, Trujillo de Extremadura, Spain

by all accounts the ruler then returned to his capital and thereafter covered in a short time the immense distance between Cuzco and Chile, where he fought many battles; certain reports suggest that he spent a whole year in that region. Departing from thence, on his return journey he first established himself in Cochabamba; to this fertile Bolivian valley he introduced many *mitimaes*, or settlers, from other parts of his empire, to cultivate the rich soil. Cochabamba thus became not only a military bastion but also a veritable breadbasket for Inca forces in the southern part of their realm. After a pilgrimage to the important shrine of Copacabana, situated on Lake Titicaca, the ruler returned to Cuzco. Following this major southward expedition, accounts of the remainder of Huayna Capac's reign dwell upon his endless struggle against the implacable tribes of Ecuador.

Reports differ as to the final extent of Huayna Capac's northern conquests, but the available evidence suggests the existence of a rather loose form of frontier more or less following the present-day border between Colombia and Ecuador. Cabello de Balboa in particular gives a vivid account of the ruler's Ecuadorian wars, which occupied the last ten years of his reign, offering an almost blow-by-blow description of these campaigns. Cabello himself spent several years in Quito before he completed his book in 1586 and had learned much from descendants of the local chieftains who surely still cherished the traditions of battles fought by their forebears.

To cite a single example of many such encounters, one of Huayna Capac's campaigns was directed against the Caranquis; his description of the final and most dramatic event in that war may serve as a good example of Cabello's lively narrative. For five whole days the Incas attacked a Caranqui fort but were unable to breach its defences. A further attempt was then planned but this was in reality only a feigned assault, and the attacking force retreated with the unsuspecting Caranquis in hot pursuit. Meanwhile, a second Inca force was able to penetrate the now unguarded fort, while a third contingent under the ruler's direct command fell upon the Caranquis who had made the sortie. Surrounded on all sides, they floundered in a marsh of reeds in which they either drowned or were slaughtered; the locality was henceforth known as Yahuarcocha, the Lake of Blood; it still features on modern maps of Ecuador. Cieza de León, when he visited Yahuarcocha, recorded eyewitness descriptions of the slaughter of 20,000 warriors in the Lake of Blood.

Having devoted the latter part of his reign to these Ecuadorian wars, Huayna Capac, after a brief visit to the coast, fell sick and died, possibly from smallpox, originally imported by earlier Spanish visitors to the New World, but which may have spread to Peru before the Spaniards themselves arrived there. The emperor's servants reportedly sent two relay teams to the great shrine of Pachacamac to ask what should be done for the health of their lord. The oracle replied through the mouth of the idol that the Inca should be taken out into the sun and that he would then get well. The advice was meticulously followed, but with the opposite result, for when the Inca was exposed to the sun he promptly died.

The Archaeological Record

Contemporary archaeological research tells us less of Inca beginnings, but serves to enrich our knowledge of the scope and extent of Inca conquest, previously based on data derived almost wholly from the written sources. It is now becoming clear after many decades of study that the more standard types of Inca pottery of imperial times, whenever found in any quantity, is a positive indication of the presence of Inca conquerors. Hence archaeology may be expected to play an ever increasing role, since much can be learned of the limits of Inca expansion by simply mapping the points where such pottery has been located. If we find Inca ceramics present in a given site but absent from a place, say, twenty kilometres to the south, then in many instances, but not always, a tentative border can be established.

Much still remains to be done in this respect and large sectors of the imperial frontier remain ill-defined, particularly in northern Peru and southern Bolivia, where tentative maps may commit errors in that respect. As a good example of current redefinition of frontiers, the coast of Ecuador may be cited, which has traditionally been treated as part of the empire. However, not only in southern Colombia, but also in coastal Ecuador, evidence of an Inca presence is scarce; Inca pottery is notable by its absence and the persistent tendency of certain chroniclers to describe coastal Ecuador as a province becomes less acceptable; reported expeditions by Inca rulers to that region were presumably excursions rather than conquests. As another example of revised conclusions might be cited the area to the west of the Bolivian city of Santa Cruz, which is now considered to have formed part of the empire, following investigation of the site of Samaipata. Equally, some light on the ultimate limits of conquest is shed by the fact that at present the southernmost of Inca remains in Chile so far discovered are the cemetery of Nos in San José de Maipo and the fortress of Chena, both situated less than twenty kilometres south of the present-day capital, Santiago.

Less well studied, but of great potential utility for the definition of boundaries, are Inca forts. As more of these are located and investigated, they may help to define for some areas the outermost Inca boundary, as well as earlier limits before subsequent expansion.

The chroniclers' accounts of the Ecuadorian wars frequently mention the use of forts. Archaeologists have now confirmed some of these accounts by discovering, for instance, no fewer than thirty-seven fortresses in the northern Ecuadorian Andes, though it is not as yet very easy to determine the identity of the builders of such constructions, where both Inca and pre-Inca pottery have been found.

Concerning the Cuzco region itself, in earlier times a series of hill sites has been studied in the vicinity of the future Inca capital with Killke pottery which may date from as early as AD 1000; one site lies literally within the precinct of the great fortress of Sacsahuaman, which guarded Cuzco. As we have seen above, recent excavations suggest that some form of Inca presence may have been established in the region long before the traditional date for their arrival, though not necessarily localized within the city of Cuzco.

In many regions fortifications formed such an integral part of the military infrastructure that their importance in Inca times might almost be compared to that of castles in European warfare in the Middle Ages. While almost no true forts have yet been found in the eastern border regions of Peru, defensive sites have been located in north-western Argentina, a region for which historical data are scant; it is not yet, however, very clear to what extent these might have been frontier posts.

As we have seen, the chroniclers' accounts of the wars of the last two great emperors tend to concentrate on their gruelling campaigns fought against the savage tribes of Ecuador, with rather scant reference to other important campaigns. The siege and capture of fortresses in Ecuador are often described in vivid terms. But the location of so many fortresses in the northern Ecuadorian Andes now lends a certain authenticity to the scope of this form of siege warfare, as described by the chroniclers.

Huascar and Atahualpa

When the Spanish conquistadors arrived, they found the Inca realm still in the throes of a convulsion that formed a tragic epilogue to its great achievements.

On Huayna Capac's death, a power struggle between rival elements again ensued. A legitimate son of Huayna Capac, Huascar, was duly enthroned in Cuzco, escorted by no fewer than forty other sons of the late ruler. However, a deep rivalry prevailed between Huascar and Atahualpa, usually described as an illegitimate offspring of the late ruler. Atahualpa initially made no bid to seize the throne, but the hostility between the two brothers was intensified as the result of the massacre of many of the nobles who accompanied Huayna Capac's body to Cuzco, and who were supporters of Atahualpa.

War ensued, in which Huascar's forces initially triumphed; his general, Atoc, marched northwards to Ecuador, occupied Tumebamba and captured Atahualpa. The latter, however, miraculously escaped from his prison by drilling a hole in a wall with a silver bar given to him by an important lady who had been allowed to visit him. The Spaniards, alas, were to prove themselves more efficient as jailers!

Following his liberation, Atahualpa assembled a large force and defeated Atoc at Ambato (to the south of Quito). Atahualpa's army then marched southwards and fought a series of engagements with Huascar's forces. Huascar's own career eventually ended on a tragic note. Awoken from his drunken slumber at midday, and warned that Atahualpa's generals, Quizquiz and Chalco Chima, were approaching Cuzco, Huascar in person precipitously set forth with a large army. But his leadership was so inept that he was defeated and captured; he was subsequently killed by his escort on Atahualpa's orders.

But as we shall later see in our final chapter, Atahualpa's triumph was short-lived. At the very moment when he was celebrating in Humachuco the news of Huascar's capture, he received the portentous tidings of the landing of a small band of exotic beings, who were already marching inland.

CHAPTER SEVEN

THE SACRED CITY

The Lion in the Mountain

Garcilasco de la Vega, describing Cuzco, writes, 'The Incas held the whole city as itself a sacred thing. It was one of their principal idols.' Cuzco was thus, in a sense, itself a *huaca*, endowed with a unique sanctity, representing for the Incas a concept as well as a city; it was often conceived as a mountain lion, lying on its right side, with the great fortress of Sacsahuaman as its head, the Río Tullumayo as its back, while its tail emerges where the rivers Tullumayu and Huatany converge. According to the chronicler Juán de Betanzos, the south-western part of the city was known as Pumap Chupan, meaning 'the lion's tail'.

As part of its symbolic aura, Cuzco was in a more literal sense the heart of their realm, since from its centre radiated the four arterial roads that led to the four *suyus*, or quarters, of the empire, collectively known in Quechua as Tahuantinsuyu.

The Cuzco of the imperial era, as seen by the Spanish invaders, was essentially created by Pachacutec, though his successors further enhanced its splendour. No plans or maps of pre-Hispanic Cuzco survive, but a few of the first Spaniards to view the city recorded their impressions. They described a city that was both refined and resplendent, yet retaining a certain pristine touch; the temples were lavishly adorned with gold, but were covered by roofs of straw. As an example, one may cite the great palace of Casana, where the conquistador Francisco Pizarro first lodged, and which had two towers of finely cut stone, surmounted by straw roofs. Slates exist in Peru, but the Incas continued to use thatch on a wooden frame. The central part of Cuzco, with its narrow winding streets, possessed a certain sombre grandeur, but lacked the great monumental vistas devised to enhance the splendour of other imperial cities. None the less, as a modern visitor, one cannot help feeling that in its narrow streets and tiny alleys one is brought closer to the true past, and even to a sense of how ancient Cuzco might really have looked, than might be the case in viewing the vestiges of imperial capitals of the Old World, or even Tenochtitlan, where the Spanish metropolis was built on the ruins of the Aztec city.

As an example one may cite one early visitor, Sancho de la Hoz, who, though impressed by the architecture of the great stone houses, remarks on the narrowness of the streets; he describes them as 'crossing

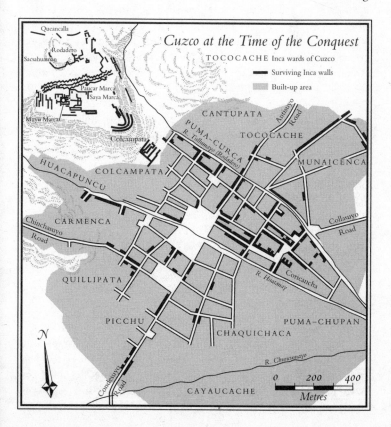

Cuzco at the Time of the Conquest

TOCOCACHE Inca wards of Cuzco

▬▬ Surviving Inca walls

░ Built-up area

Qucancalla

Rodadero

Sacsahuaman

Paucar Marca
Saya Marca

Muyu Marca

Colcampata

CANTUPATA

PUMA-CURCA

R. Tullumayo (Rodadero)

TOCOCACHE

Antisuyo Road

MUNAICENCA

HUACAPUNCU

COLCAMPATA

CARMENCA

Chinchasuyo Road

Collasuyo Road

QUILLIPATA

R. Huatanay

Coricancha

PICCHU

PUMA-CHUPAN

CHAQUICHACA

R. Chunchunayo

CAYAUCACHE

Condesuyo Road

N

0   200   400
Metres

at right angles, very straight, all paved with stone and in the middle of each one runs a water channel lined with stone. Their defect is in being narrow, since only a single horseman can go on one side of the channel and another on the other side.'

In spite of the comments of de la Hoz, the Spaniards, themselves accustomed to cramped cities of mediaeval structure, which even retained certain Muslim traits, sought to make few changes in the original plan, except to reduce the great open space formed by the two principal squares of Aucaypata and Cusipata.

Apart from the division into four *suyus*, formed by the four great converging roads, the city was curiously endowed with a system of notional lines called *ceques*, that emanated like the spokes of a wheel from a central point, the great temple enclosure of Coricancha. The *ceque* system conformed to an ancient Andean tendency to express concepts in linear terms, present in Nazca and present also among many Andean groups, including the Aymara peoples of the Lake Titicaca region.

In all there were forty-one *ceques*, or notional lines, in Cuzco, mainly radiating from the Temple of the Sun. Dr Tom Zuidema is the author of important studies which stress the extreme complexity of the system. On the forty-one *ceques* were situated no fewer than 328 *huacas*, or sacred stones, together with numerous sanctuaries. The *ceques* were not only important to Inca religion, but also basic to the calendrical system. A puzzling aspect is their relation to the *panacas*, the households of defunct rulers, on an ostensibly arbitrary basis, since Pachacutec's *panaca* was generously endowed, while his successor, Tupac, was identified with a single *ceque*.

The Two Cuzcos

Fundamental both to the layout and to the general concept of Cuzco was the existence within the city of two moieties, Hanan (upper) and Hurin (lower) Cuzco, the latter being situated in the south-eastern part, in the area where the Tullumayu and Huatany rivers converge. As we have already seen, Manco and his immediate successors reportedly resided in the temple enclosure of Coricancha, situated in Hurin, and the division into two halves is attributed to Inca Roca, the sixth ruler. Thenceforth the monarchs lived in Hanan, where each erected his own palace. These were built on a grandiose scale, complete with reception halls that could hold up to 3000 people. They were provided with elaborate plumbing, and each palace had its own bathing establishment with hot and cold water which flowed along stone channels.

Such a division into Hurin and Hanan, far from being an innovation, was most widespread and existed in many regions as distant one from another as the Lupaqa principalities of Lake Titicaca and the highlands of central Ecuador. While certain scholars suggest that the Incas might have imposed the system on parts of their vast realm where it had not existed before, the Hurin–Hanan division, like so many other aspects of their rule, would seem to have dated from pre-Inca times.

The division of Cuzco into two halves lies at the very root of its system of government, since from the time of Inca Roca onwards Hanan Cuzco assumed a certain primacy in war and secular government, whereas Hurin, where Coricancha and countless other temples and shrines were situated, was the seat of religious hierarchy.

The division into Hurin and Hanan has led certain authors to pose the question as to whether the two Cuzcos, upper and lower, might have been ruled not by one, but by two dynasties, as occurred, for instance, among the Lupaqa, who at the time of the *Visita* of Garci Díez de San Miguel in 1567 were still divided into two halves, Hanansaya and Hurinsaya, governed respectively by rulers named Cari and Cusi. In Cuzco, notwithstanding any political primacy of Hanan, the traditional hierarchy of Hurin Cuzco clearly retained much influence, exercised for instance in their support of Huascar in the civil war against Atahualpa, just before the Conquest.

Fundamental to Pachacutec's rebuilding of Cuzco was an ambitious programme of public works, based on the canalization of the two rivers, whose flooding in the rainy season was a constant menace, and frequently inundated the city. The chronicler Juán de Betanzos describes the elaborate infrastructure; having studied the problem in detail, Pachacu-tec convoked the local lords, ordering them to gather in Cuzco, bringing copious provisions and ample manpower. The work involved a process of canalization, leading as far as Mohina, four leagues below the conflu-ence of the two rivers. Large quantities of coarse stone were required to complete the task. True to local tradition, these labours were preceded by five days of ritual feasting; after the whole work was completed further festivities followed, lasting six days and involving the consumption of lavish quantities of *chicha* and coca, accompanied by a presentation of gifts.

As we have already seen, Pachacutec revamped the great temple enclosure of Coricancha, which had also served as the residence of the early Inca rulers, whose cult was an essential feature of the shrine. A portion of Coricancha survives today in the form of the curving wall beneath the western end of the Church of Santo Domingo. The first Spaniards to arrive in Cuzco found the buildings of the temple still sheathed in gold; they themselves were forced to strip the gold with copper crowbars, since no Indian was willing to assist. In all, 700 plates from Coricancha were included in the gold sent to the north; the plates averaged two kilos in weight.

The walls of Coricancha were constructed of 'coursed' masonry, in which rectangular blocks are laid in even horizontal courses. A further example of this elaborate process still visible today is the site of the Acllahuasi, the home of the Inca's chosen women, and now the convent of Santa Catalina. Every visitor to Cuzco is shown the stone of Hatun Rumiyoc; this was part of a construction built by the 'polygonal' method, a form of tightly fitting masonry used by the Incas for their principal buildings; the famous stone has no fewer than twelve corners on its outer face; in this elaborate Inca polygonal masonry the stones simply interlock, with the convex part of one stone fitting exactly into the concave form of the other. Such stonecutting skills recall those of earlier times in the region of Lake Titicaca and in particular the great ruins of Tiahuanaco.

Though its completion was the work of successive sovereigns, Pachacutec's establishment of the great fortress of Sacsahuaman also involved major feats of organization. Cieza de León writes that the basic task required a labour force of 20,000 men. These labourers worked only for a limited period, after which they were relieved by others. Four thousand men broke the stones, while 6000 bore them to the site and others dug the deep foundations. The workers were housed in nearby buildings, whose walls were still visible in Cieza's time. He comments on the vast size and weight of the blocks of stone, many of which can be seen today. He further confirms that Tupac Inca, Huayna Capac and even Huascar continued the work.

A modern visitor may share the amazement of the first Spanish visitors that stones of such a size could apparently have been conveyed to Cuzco from a distant quarry and then assembled into a complex jigsaw, still partly visible. Modern geologists, incidentally, disagree with Garcilasco and Cieza and suggest that most of the material for Sacsahuaman was quarried a hundred metres north of the hill itself. The edifice was built to serve as a storehouse as much as a fort, and the Spaniards were astonished by the massive quantities of fine jewels, gold and silver which they found there. It was also important as a shrine, serving as a temple to the sun that almost rivalled Coricancha.

Basic to the general layout of the city was the great open space created by the two contiguous plazas, Aucaypata and Cusipata. Today Cusipata has been built over while Aucaypata became the Plaza de Armas and survives as the main square. Originally Aucaypata was reserved for the principal religious festivals, whereas Cusipata was the scene of military ceremonies and parades. Many palaces of the Hanan-based rulers were built on Aucaypata. On the north side was Cuyusmanco, situated where the cathedral now stands; in this building the Spaniards took refuge during the rebellion of Manco Inca. On the north-west side of the square were two great structures, Casana and Coracora. Casana was the largest palace, reportedly built by Pachacutec. Its outstanding feature was a huge hall of wooden columns. Garcilasco de la Vega saw it when he was a boy: 'In many of the houses of the Incas there were vast halls that were still intact in Cuzco during my childhood.' (He was born in 1539.) 'The largest was Casana, which was capable of holding four thousand people.' The great hall of Casana was later destroyed to make way for colonial arcades and shops. On the opposite side of the square lay Huayna Capac's palace, Amaru Cancha, with a great gateway of multicoloured marble. Sancho de la Hoz describes it as the most impressive of the palaces on the square. The Jesuits' fine pink baroque church of La Companía now occupies its site.

In describing the buildings of central Cuzco, the heart of the city, it is important to bear in mind that only the nobility and their servants, the *yanas*, together with members of the religious hierarchy, were privileged to live within its confines.

Various chroniclers confirm that the Incas by privilege, as opposed to the *orejones*, or original nobles, were not allowed to reside in central Cuzco. They lived beyond the triangle bounded by the two rivers. Their dwellings, less elaborate than those of inner Cuzco, were separated from the latter by a stretch of open land. In contrast to the stone mansions of the old nobility, Cieza states that such houses were made of straw and wood and little trace of them survives. He makes the perhaps surprising comment that most of the city was inhabited by *mitimaes*, those countless settlers imported from conquered provinces, after many of the original inhabitants of this outer Cuzco had been transferred to remoter regions, as a means of establishing firm Inca control over newly conquered peoples.

Outer Cuzco was thus an extensive area of dwellings, housing both the Incas by privilege and countless artisans and technicians. Estimates vary widely as to the total population; while the centre of the city, the home of the elite, was clearly not large, by some accounts containing about 10,000 houses, the conquistador Sancho de la Hoz calculated that the whole Valley of Cuzco contained 100,000 houses, but such a figure may have included many dwellings that lay well beyond the confines of even the outer city.

The Gods of Cuzco

Viracocha, as we have already seen, was the traditional creator deity. Closely associated with the shores of Lake Titicaca, he rose from the lake when all was dark and created, or re-created, the sun and moon. He then killed the previous inhabitants and fashioned new people out of stone, among whom were the fledgling Incas, whom he led to the Valley of Cuzco.

Viracocha is indisputably cast by the chroniclers in the role of the creator of all things. But they offer rather enigmatic interpretations of the degree to which this creator god retained the rank of supreme deity or whether, alternatively, he relinquished control of the world that he had fashioned to the sky gods, among whom the primordial deity was Inti, the sun, worshipped as the divine ancestor of the Inca dynasty.

A clear understanding of Inca religion is hard to attain since we depend on the writings of sixteenth-century priests and conquistadors, obsessed with the salvation of the pagan world through Christianity, a notion wholly meaningless to their native informants. They were thus ill-disposed to probe the subtleties of Inca religious thought. These chroniclers tended to reinterpret and westernize concepts gleaned from their informants and which were wholly alien to them. As a result, a tendency prevailed to 'pigeon-hole' Andean deities and to regard each god or goddess as associated with certain specific functions, linked to well-defined facets of human life.

John Rowe is foremost among the scholars who first sought to interpret the chroniclers' accounts; he goes so far as to suggest that the Inca creation myth was a late compilation, introduced into their religion by Pachacutec, as part of his process of religious reform, which thus tended to modify the role of their tribal deity, Inti, the sun god, thereby reduced to the role of a mere son of the supreme creator. Other scholars, on the contrary, tend to stress the supremacy of Inti and to portray Viracocha as little more than an 'otiose high god'.

However, as Arthur Demarest has insisted in his study of the Andean high god, the most splendid ceremonies seem to honour the sun rather than Viracocha, and the priest of Inti, the sun, presides at all important rituals. The Inca himself confessed his sins not to Viracocha, but directly to the sun and the sun god is generally described as the father of the Incas. Moreover, it is Inti who inspired the cult of the Inca ruler as the conqueror and titular owner of vast realms in whose main centres the Incas invariably built a temple to honour the worship of the sun.

In all accounts an important place in the Inca pantheon is also assigned to the Inca thunder, or weather, god, Illapa. Illapa, in his role as rain giver, was greatly revered and many temples were dedicated to his worship. His image was displayed beside that of Inti in the great square in Cuzco and his effigy was carried in processions in a gold-encrusted litter.

According to almost every chronicler, the creator, sun and weather gods shared the main altar in the Temple of the Sun in the Coricancha temple complex. They are pictured together on the altar in the drawings of Huaman Poma. Moreover, their images invariably figured in the major religious ceremonies.

The Inca hierarchical establishment was, at least in theory, massively endowed as the owner of part of the lands in each conquered province. At the head of this establishment stood the High Priest of Coricancha, the very centre of the imperial cult, where Pachacutec placed effigies of past rulers, seated on golden thrones. Their mummified remains were jealously guarded by their *panacas*.

As part of his religious reform, Pachacutec had also introduced the cult of the 'Young Sun', Punchao, to whom he dedicated another magnificent statue of solid gold, housed in its own temple.

Central to the functioning of the great temple complex were the Virgins of the Sun, called Acllacona in Quechua, simply meaning 'chosen women'. The name was apt since the process of selection was rigorous. During a novitiate of three years practical tasks were learned, such as cooking and spinning; when they reached the age of about fifteen the High Priest, accompanied by the Inca in person, went to the temple and commanded them to choose between marriage to a noble and dedication to the service of the sun.

Each principal Inca centre throughout the provinces had its Acllacona convent, subject to the authority of a woman revered as the bride of the sun god. The largest of these establishments, that of the great temple complex in Cuzco, consisted of more than 1500 women. Among their many tasks was the preparation of ceremonial food and of the drink *chicha*, consumed in vast quantities during feasts. The exquisite garments woven by these women were designed for the ruler and his family, as well as for leading priests; some were used in sacrificial ceremonies. Rigorous chastity was imposed on the Virgins of the Sun; if this rule was infringed, they were buried alive.

Inca Rituals

The virgins played a leading role in Inca ceremonial, of which vivid accounts survive, some deriving from Spanish eyewitnesses. Pachacutec was reportedly the author of Inca ceremonialism in its most spectacular form; under his guidance the calendar of monthly ceremonies was redesigned in such a way as to dramatize the spiritual life of the people and to reinforce the imperial cult.

Basic to this purpose was the initial ceremony which took place in

December and was known as Capac Raymi (the Great Festival), which involved rigorous tests of endurance as a preliminary to the initiation of the young nobles.

After gruelling nights of exposure on the icy slopes of a nearby peak, the boys came down to Cuzco; having performed a special dance they were whipped on their arms and legs by their more seasoned kinsmen. Only on the fourteenth day did they again climb the slopes of another mountain. This ascent was followed by a headlong downhill race that sometimes caused maiming and even death. The same process was then repeated twice over; the bizarre ritual of the ascent and descent of the four mountains perhaps symbolized the fourfold division of Tahuantin-suyu. On the twenty-first day the boys were richly attired and then their earlobes were split in preparation for the insertion of the earplugs, the ceremony which would formally confer on them the appellation of *orejón*.

The most sumptuous feast was the Inti Raymi, to celebrate the harvesting of the maize crop in June. The Spaniards, as part of the policy of placating their puppet emperor, Manco, before he finally revolted, allowed the Incas to perform some of their great rituals, of a kind that had been immediately suppressed in post-Conquest Mexico. Hence we have a European eyewitness description of Inti Raymi from Cristóbal de Molina, a Spanish priest. After the initial sacrifices by the Inca himself, the effigies, or mummies, of the former rulers were brought out and placed under finely worked feather awnings. They were accompanied by richly robed *orejones* wearing silver cloaks and tunics. As the sun rose, they began to chant in splendid harmony and unison. The Inca, seated on a rich stool beneath a canopy, was the first to open the chant.

In the words of Cristóbal de Molina, 'Throughout this time great offerings were being made. On a platform on which there was a tree, there were Indians doing nothing but throwing meats into a great fire and burning them up in it. At another place the Inca ordered ewes [llamas] to be thrown for the poorer common Indians to grab, and this caused great sport.

'At eight o'clock over two hundred girls came out of Cuzco, each with a large new pot of one and a half *arrobas* (twenty-seven litres) of *chicha*, plastered and with a cover. The girls came in groups of five, full of precision and order, and pausing at intervals. They also offered to the sun many bales of a herb that the Indians chew and call coca, whose leaf is like myrtle.

'There were many other ceremonies and sacrifices. It is sufficient to say that when the sun was about to set in the evening the Indians showed great sadness at its departure, in their chants and expressions. They allowed their voices to die away on purpose. And as the sun was sinking completely and disappearing from sight they made a great act of reverence, raising their hands and worshipping it in the deepest humility. All the apparatus of the festival was immediately dismantled and the canopies were removed. Everyone returned to their homes and the effigies and fearsome relics were returned to their houses and shrines.

'These effigies that they had under the awnings were those of former Incas who had ruled Cuzco. Each had a great retinue of men who stayed there all day fanning away flies with fans like hand mirrors, made of swans' feathers. Each also had its *mamaconas*, who are like nuns: there were some twelve to fifteen in each awning.

'They came out in this same way for eight or nine days in succession. When all the festivals were over, they brought out on the last day many hand ploughs – these had formerly been made of gold. After the religious service the Inca took a plough and began to break the earth, and the rest of the lords did the same. Following their lead the entire kingdom did likewise. No Indian would have dared to break the earth until the Inca had done so, and none believed that the earth could produce unless the Inca broke it first.'

This ritual breaking of the earth by the Inca was the means of asserting his personal authority throughout his domains. Sacrifice was basic to Inca ceremonial. The most usual offerings were those of llamas and guinea pigs, offered in profusion to many *huacas*. Brown llamas were sacrificed to Viracocha, white llamas and alpacas to the sun. The priest led the animal around the image, then turned its head towards the god and slit its throat. Food and *chicha* were also regularly presented as sacrificial offerings to the *huacas* and to the mummies of former rulers.

Human sacrifice, often treated more as a monopoly of the ancient Mexicans, was not infrequent. In certain instances when a new province was conquered, a few of the most handsome inhabitants were brought to Cuzco and offered to the sun in thanks for victory. While sacrifice was hardly practised on a mass scale, men, women, and above all children, were offered whenever a special appeal to the mercy of the gods was called for; this might occur at the beginning of a new reign, if the ruler was gravely ill, if an earthquake occurred, or some other natural calamity faced the empire. In outlying provinces human sacrifice was also practised. Children were required for the Inca temples; they had to be physically perfect, without marks or blemishes. They were feasted before sacrifice that they might not die hungry or unhappy; older children were usually first made drunk. Some of them were buried alive, but most were forced to walk three times round the image of the god, after which their throats were cut or their hearts torn out; while still beating, the hearts were offered to the god. The bodies were buried in special cemeteries near important shrines, such as Pachacamac, where the contents of such burial grounds have been studied by archaeologists. Sacrifice, mainly of children and white llamas, was also used for the purpose of divination, a very key element in Inca religious practice. The Incas believed in the need to consult the forces of the supernatural before taking any important action, particularly with regard to military operations. For such purposes certain important shrines were used, including Pachacamac and also Apurimac, situated on the banks of the Río Apurimac near Cuzco.

Divination of a more everyday nature was accomplished by observing the movements of snakes and spiders. According to Bernabé Cobo, in central and northern Peru, when a diviner was consulted, he would open a large jar containing a live spider; if any of its legs were bent, it was a bad augury. Evil omens tended to outnumber good ones. Eclipses and falling stars foretold disasters such as the death of an emperor. When a comet appeared during the imprisonment of Atahualpa at Cajamarca, he concluded (not incorrectly) that his end was near. Even such natural phenomena as the hooting of an owl or the howling of a dog were held to foretell the death of a relative.

To encounter snakes, lizards, spiders, toads and even big worms was an evil omen. If a snake was found in a house, the owner killed it, urinated upon it, and then crushed it with his left foot to ward off evil.

Notions of the afterlife, usually so basic to religious practice, were somewhat vague. Virtuous persons went to live with the sun in the upper world, while sinners went to the interior of the Earth, where they had no food but stones. The nobles, however, were spared such privations and supposedly went to heaven regardless of their virtues.

The Sapan Inca

The ruler, officially known as the Sapan Inca, was supreme in both spiritual and temporal affairs. But, notwithstanding his sublime status, the procedure by which he attained it is rather ill-defined. Most chroniclers, imbued with European notions of primogeniture, erroneously assumed that the ruler's eldest son became his rightful heir.

The Polish scholar Mariusz Ziolkowski deduces from the available data that in earlier times the High Priest, as the mouthpiece of the sun, was directly responsible for the choice of a new sovereign, whose election took place in Coricancha. To the question as to who in turn chose the High Priest, no clear answer exists. But according to the same author, following Pachacutec's religious reformation, roles were reversed; the High Priest was henceforth nominated by the sovereign, while the choice of ruler was simply made by 'the lords of Cuzco', who chose the most apt of the late monarch's kin.

As the empire expanded, each succession was marked by a struggle for power. The number of potential candidates to the throne was in theory limited to the children of a single royal spouse, known as the *coya* (queen), often in later times a sister of the new ruler, whom he married on the day that he received the royal tassel. However, some *coyas* produced no heirs, while others had several sons who then became rival claimants, leading to a fierce struggle for power whenever the throne became vacant.

A further procedure was introduced as a means to eliminate strife: the adoption of one heir as co-ruler during a king's lifetime. But this practice also tended to fail, since rulers were apt to change their minds and substitute a second co-ruler for their original choice, thus fomenting the likelihood of bitter conflict between these successive co-rulers on their father's death. Pachacutec, for instance, chose Amaru Yupanqui, but later adopted Tupac Yupanqui in his place. Tupac, the favourite candidate of the military rather than the religious hierarchy, was then confronted with a palace revolt, fomented by yet another brother after his succession. Tupac himself never designated an official co-ruler but altered his original choice as successor, naming when already on his death bed, Titu Cusi, son of his sister–wife, Mama Ocllo. Only after a bitter internal feud did Titu Cusi prevail and succeed to the throne, assuming the name of Huayna Capac.

Hence it becomes clear that disputes over the succession were not confined to the ultimate and most disastrous instance, the civil war between Atahualpa and Huascar; the latter was to some extent the preferred choice of the religious hierarchy of Lower Cuzco, while Atahualpa was the favourite of the northern armies.

In spite of such initial impediments, the Inca monarch, once duly enthroned, was an absolute ruler, whose authority was unquestioned. An aura of divinity enhanced his role as the offspring of the sun. This association with Inti, the solar deity, was part of the cult that united not only the empire, but the whole universe, since Tahuantinsuyu was conceived as corresponding with the universe itself.

The Inca's formal insignia of authority, the equivalent of a European crown, consisted of a many-coloured braid band wound several times round the head, from which hung a red fringe with tassels fixed to little golden tubes. The emperor, as part of his insignia, on important occasions carried a mace with a golden star-head. He travelled in a litter with an immense following and his dignity required him to proceed as slowly as possible, not more than about twelve miles a day. Anyone who sought audience, no matter what his rank, had to remove his sandals and place a token burden upon his back; the ruler usually sat behind a screen and only in exceptional instances received visitors face to face.

The semi-divine status of the later rulers was enhanced by the presence of a protective band of women, including secondary wives, who produced a large number of offspring, many of whom played a leading role in civil and above all military affairs. By Atahualpa's time, according to his sister, Ines Yupanqui, the ruler's wives were held in such high esteem that no one even dared to look them in the face; however, a wife who committed any impropriety would immediately be killed.

John Hemming in his account of the Spanish Conquest describes the Spanish fascination with the elaborate rituals that formed part of the Inca monarch's fastidious existence, even in captivity. To quote

Pedro Pizarro, 'When Atahualpa ate, he was seated on a wooden stool little more than a span [twenty centimetres] high. This stool was of very lovely reddish wood and was always kept covered with a delicate rug, even when he was seated upon it. The ladies brought his meal and placed it before him on tender thin green rushes . . . They placed all the vessels of gold, silver and pottery on these rushes. He pointed to whatever he fancied and it was brought. One of the ladies took it and held it in her hand while he ate. He was eating one day in this way when I was present. A slice of food was being lifted to his mouth when a drop fell on to the clothing he was wearing. Giving his hand to the Indian lady, he rose and went to his chamber to change his dress and returned wearing a dark brown tunic and cloak. I approached him and felt the cloak, which was softer than silk. I said to him: "Inca, of what is a robe as soft as this made?" . . . He explained that it was from the skins of vampire bats that fly by night in Puerto Viejo and Tumbez and that bite the natives.'

On another occasion Pedro Pizarro was taken to see the royal storehouses, full of leather chests. Some of these contained all his discarded clothing. Others held the rushes that they placed before his feet when he ate, as well as the bones of animals or birds that he had eaten. All these items had to be burned, since everything that had been touched by the rulers, as sons of the sun, had to be reduced to ashes and thrown to the air, for no one else was allowed to touch it.

Adulation of the emperor went to sublime lengths. Another witness, Juán Ruiz de Arce, recalls that he did not expectorate on to the ground. A woman held out her hand and he spat into it. The women removed any hairs that fell on to his clothing and ate them; this was because he was frightened of sorcery and feared he might be bewitched by the hairs if they were not eaten. So profound was the respect accorded to the ruler that even when he was a Spanish prisoner chiefs from many provinces would present themselves before him, kissing his hands and feet. 'He behaved towards them in a most princely manner, showing no less majesty when imprisoned and defeated than he had before that occurred.'

Since the monarch enjoyed a semi-divine status, his death was the occasion of elaborate rites, in which the whole empire took part. His favourite women were expected to accompany him to the next world;

they were made drunk before being strangled. His elaborately wrapped body was deposited in his palace under the care of his descendants.

By virtue of this concept of the spiritual deathlessness of an Inca ruler, he passed on to his successor only the exercise of his office, not his riches. This wealth, at least in the time of Pachacutec if not before, was, as we have seen, immediately locked away within the institution known as his *panaca*, which included his blood relatives and retainers. The *panaca* began to function as soon as a ruler died; his mummy bundle, splendidly housed, was meticulously attended throughout the day; his concubines even served him his favourite foods as if he were still alive. His coca plantations continued to function, baling the finest leaves for the former ruler's use, while his shepherds continued to furnish their tallies of newborn llamas in his herds. The royal mummy even had voices, speaking through the oracular lips of his representatives, through whom he could converse with the living, at times toasting other deceased rulers and at others issuing invitations bidding them to visit him in his palace.

The *panaca* system created many internal problems, both political and economic. The huge landholdings of the *panacas*, consisting of much the best land in the Valley of Cuzco, were a fund of wealth that was frozen in time, inalienable and stagnant. A new ruler, for whom this wealth was inviolate, had to create his own patrimony, to provide for his needs and to endow his own future *panaca*. The means by which a living ruler could accumulate such riches is far from clear; Inca lands throughout the provinces were more state than personal property and it was surely hard for the ruler to obtain private lands nearer home, since much of the best land around Cuzco, apart from the *panaca* property, belonged to the royal *ayllus*. The Cuzco *ayllu* system comprised not only these eleven royal *ayllus*, but also others, probably twelve in number, that embraced the Incas by privilege, living beyond the bounds of central Cuzco.

The *ayllu*, a kinship group that still exists in present-day Peru, is somewhat hard to define and the chroniclers' accounts do little to clarify its role. John Rowe, rejecting the description of the *ayllu* as a clan, defines it as a kin group with descent in the male line, whose main function was the ownership of a defined territory.

The Señores of Cuzco

The chroniclers often refer to the choice of a new ruler as being made by the 'señores of Cuzco', by implication the *orejones*. Their status was in every respect unique, since only these nobles, together with the *yanas* who served them, could live in the central part of the city; they alone wore sumptuous clothing. The sons of *orejones* were educated in a special school.

The antecedents of this ruling class are not wholly clear. Since the emperor possessed a plethora of secondary wives, in addition to the principal spouse (the *coya*), each ruler could engender a large number of offspring. But while the *orejones* were all theoretically of royal blood, in the course of a few centuries the rulers alone could scarcely have produced enough children to form more than the nucleus of a force able to conquer a huge empire. Hence the importance of the role of the Incas by privilege, not of royal blood, but who may have been very numerous, far outnumbering the original *orejones*.

The role of the *orejones* as army commanders is clearly paramount. Close relatives, whether uncles, brothers or sons of rulers, are often named as leading generals and also as provincial governors. However, while distinctions between the exercise of military leadership and civil administration are often blurred, *orejones* surely presided over the imperial infrastructure as a whole, including such matters as irrigation, town planning and road construction.

The evidence suggests that the key posts of government were held by *orejones*, though doubtless Incas by privilege also played a major role in the administration. But when the sources often write of the 'Lords of Cuzco' or 'the Highest in the Land', as deciding key issues, particularly the succession to the throne, they presumably refer to the *orejones*.

Reports of how the Inca state functioned are hardly explicit. While certain sources write of a council of twelve who advised the ruler, references are more frequent to the presence of four counsellors, one from each of the four *suyus*, on whose advice the emperor depended for major decisions. They apparently had power to resolve all but the most difficult questions without even consulting the Inca, and played a leading role in deciding when to wage war.

But quite apart from any such inner council, whether formed of twelve or four principal *orejones* to control the Inca realm which extended over such vast distances, some form of central administrative staff was clearly needed. Modern authors often refer to this as the Inca 'bureaucracy', though the term, derived from the word for a writing desk, hardly retains the same meaning in a context where writing, and therefore paperwork, was absent.

It must always be borne in mind that, particularly in the reign of Huayna Capac, the Inca himself was continually waging war in remote parts of Ecuador and even Chile, and many pressing decisions had to be made in Cuzco that could not be referred to the ruler, notwithstanding the fine communications network. A rebellion, or perhaps an ecological disaster in, say, Collao, would require immediate action, including perhaps the mobilization and dispatch of armies. This was complicated by a special factor; unlike certain ancient empires in which the army was recruited more from the metropolitan region, the Incas deployed numerous levies drawn from peoples located throughout the length and breadth of their far-flung realm. The deployment over vast distances of such forces, and their arrival at the right time, at the right place, must have involved military staff work of a complex nature.

The infrastructure of the imperial road system must also have involved a constant process of decision making at the centre, as well as personnel capable of making detailed plans. While no records of charts or maps have survived, the question arises as to how far decisions on an imperial scale could be made without some records of this kind, since it seems almost beyond the capacity of the human brain to memorize the whole road system and all its details, including every bridge.

A key instrument of provincial rule was the decimal system, which would surely be unmanageable without the aid of the *quipu* knots, used to record numbers, but hardly events. Little detailed evidence survives of how the system functioned, though Cieza de León affirms that officials, known as *quipocamayos*, resided in each province and used the *quipus* to keep a tally of the available manpower and material resources. Cieza cites as an example the methods whereby the *quipocamayos* of the province of Xauxa displayed their talents; for instance, from their records in the form of *quipu* knots they were able to itemize the exact quantities of gold, silver, textiles, food and animals extracted by the Spaniards from that province. Similar skills obviously served to keep records of garrisons, stores and all other aspects of imperial administration, whether civil or military, and such records, not confined to purely local use, presumably required a central staff to coordinate data from each province, a process on which the decisions of the ruler (or of others in the case of his frequent absence) had to be based. Of such aspects of Inca administration, of scarce interest to Spanish chroniclers, few, if any, details survive.

Everyday Life in Cuzco

Up to this point our account of Cuzco has been centred upon the privileged classes, whose control over both the military and civil organization was absolute. Most of the chroniclers' information refers much more to such people than to the lives of the average citizen.

Bernabé Cobo stresses that this elite was far from being restricted to the Incas by blood: 'After these [the *orejones*] the governors, captains, *caciques*, and judges of the Inca, along with their children, enjoyed the immunities and exemptions of nobles; not only were they all exempt from the taxes paid by the common people, but they received salaries from their king and were supported with the tribute of personal service that the taxpayers rendered to them.'

Notwithstanding this sharp distinction that Cobo makes between the rich and the 'common people', he at least implies the existence of many different categories among the latter. In particular he mentions the craftsmen, who, as a reward for their skills, were in a sense also privileged, since they surely received more than the average person, who simply paid tribute in the form of labour: 'In place of paying tribute, the craftsmen worked in the service of the Inca, of the Church or of their own *caciques*; each one performed the craft that he knew, such as making garments, working gold or silver, extracting these metals from the mines and processing them, making clay and wooden cups, as well as practising other crafts.' The chronicler, however, goes on to say that these craftsmen were provided with tools and instruments, and did not invest anything of their own except manual labour.

The *queros*, or wooden cups, mentioned above, are among the most characteristic forms of Inca art, which in some respects tends to be regarded as rather pedestrian as compared with that of earlier Peruvian cultures. Some types of *quero* were carved in the shape of a puma's or jaguar's head and others in the form of a man's head. Most are inlaid with lacquer, with geometric designs, arranged in zones, cut into their surface. These Inca-style wooden cups continued to be made in the Colonial period, depicting not only Indians in Hispanicized dress but also Spaniards. As John Rowe observes, the designs on these cups are superb and their illustrations of battle scenes, hunting, expeditions to the eastern forests, dances and festivals, plants and animals, illustrate nearly every aspect of the life of that period; Rowe even compares them to the best work of the Mexican codices!

While the aesthetic appeal of their pottery is indeed hardly comparable

Figure 30 Inca Goblet or Quero *from Ollantaytambo*

to that of certain earlier cultures, late Inca ware, if unimaginative, is distinctive. Inca pottery is fine-grained, very hard, and finished with a polished surface; the decoration is characterized by a constant repetition of geometric patterns: diamonds, chequers and cross-hatching. Life forms are seldom used, while colours are rather sombre with red, black and white prevailing. Such pottery, as we have seen, was widely diffused throughout the empire, offering to the archaeologist concrete evidence as to its extent.

In contrast to the splendour of Inca palaces and temples, the dwellings of the common people were so simple as to lead Bernabé Cobo to affirm that they should really be called huts or cabins rather than houses. The walls were of beaten earth, or, on the coast, of adobe bricks. They had no windows and no chimney, the smoke from the fire escaping through the thatched roof; the simple entrance was low and small. These simple, one-storey constructions contained a single room in which a whole family lived, cooked, and slept, with the floor serving both as table and bed. Llama skins, thrown on the ground and folded double, took the place of beds, one half serving as mattress and the other half as a covering.

In these modest habitations the family seldom gathered until after nightfall. Either they were scattered due to their various occupations, or else remained crouched on the threshold. Their austere mode of life was closely monitored by the authorities; the houses were inspected by officials twice a year, and the hanging over the doorway had to be open at mealtimes, in order that inspectors could verify that all the rules were being observed.

The garments worn by the common people were almost as simple as their dwellings. On the chilly *altiplano* clothing was a necessity, while on the coast it was needed only to cover certain sensitive parts of the body. The typical Inca man's dress consisted of a breechcloth and a sleeveless tunic, with a large cloak for cold weather and for more formal occasions. The sleeveless tunic consisted of a long piece of cloth with a slit in the middle for the head; it reached nearly to the knees. At higher altitudes such garments were made of llama wool; once this everyday robe was put on, it lasted until it was worn out.

Women would wear a long, belted tunic, open at the sides and freeing the legs for ease in walking; they also wore grey cloaks, fastened across the breast by a large-headed pin. Both sexes usually went barefoot, but sometimes wore sandals with soles made of llama leather; such sandals had a brightly coloured woollen fastening.

While the sources tend to ascribe to the living conditions of the working masses a certain uniformity, the number of a man's wives rather than the nature of his dwelling was perhaps a better index of his wealth and prestige, though the majority of the common people were probably too poor to possess more than one wife, since polygamy ranked as a sign of wealth. In all cases the first wife took precedence over subsequent spouses; many of the latter were war captives with whom the Inca regaled his more deserving subjects. Such secondary wives could not take the place of the first wife if she died; if their husband died, the secondary wives could be inherited by a son.

The ordinary Inca families lived in groups for which still today the term *ayllu* is used. In modern Indian society, the *ayllu* consists of a number of unrelated extended families living together in a restricted area and following certain rules of crop rotation. There is no doubt that comparable systems existed in ancient times, but their exact nature is hard to define. It is important to bear in mind that in outer Cuzco, beyond the traditional and closely clustered centre, conditions were not so strictly urban, and cultivation of the available land played an important role in people's lives. John Rowe insists, as we have seen, that the *ayllu* in Inca times was not a clan in the strictest sense, but a kind of kin group with, at least in theory, descent from a common male ancestor, and control of a definite territory of which each family cultivated a part. In Inca times these family lots were redistributed every year in conformity with changing needs.

Bernabé Cobo in writing of Inca marriage deprecates the lack of interest in the chastity of the bride: 'We should pass over rapidly such a foul smelling quagmire, the sewer of turpitude and indecency in which these idolaters wallowed . . . Because they never knew the splendour and beauty of chastity, they never appreciated it. They said that those who were virgins had never been loved by anyone. As a matter of fact few remained virgins until they were married . . . In accord with such depraved customs, when an Indian chooses a woman to be his wife, he does not try to find out if she has led a virtuous life. The foremost consideration was the wealth that she possessed; second to this was her capacity for hard work. Since this second question could only be determined by trial and error, a man would usually first take a woman as a concubine and keep her on a trial basis for months, or even at times for years!'

While this attitude towards sexual behaviour might seem distinctly lax, in other respects the children were subject to precise rules and strict discipline. When a child reached a certain age, which varied in different regions between five and twelve years, he was integrated into the group with a ritual cutting of hair and nails. An even more formal ceremony took place at between age twelve and fourteen years, when the child was incorporated into the *ayllu* and into the nation. The elders whipped the legs of a young man, and reminded him of his duty towards his parents and his superiors.

Except perhaps on the numerous feast days, the diet of the unprivileged was rather austere. Two meals were served a day, in the early morning and at sunset. The dishes were placed on the floor, where the man and his wife sat back to back, eating from separate plates, into which guinea pigs and dogs would thrust their noses at will. The most basic food, known as *chuno*, was made from potatoes, simply ground and mixed with water, salt and pepper, to form a kind of gruel. As an alternative, maize was roasted, boiled, or ground into flour. The popular diet seems to have been somewhat lacking in protein; llamas were not generally eaten, but used exclusively to provide wool and as a means of transport. Guinea pigs were domesticated, but were only edible for twelve hours after being killed. Birds, frogs and even worms were used to flavour soups.

From the rather scanty information available, one gains the impression that the diet of the ordinary people, as opposed to the upper classes, was somewhat low not only in protein but calories, particularly in view of the heavy work that they were expected to perform. It has, however, to be borne in mind that much of our information on such matters derives from Cobo, who wrote over a century after the Conquest and based his information mainly on his own observation of how the common people lived in his day rather than in pre-Conquest times; the earlier chroniclers, such as Cieza de León and Juán de Betanzos, offer little information on such matters as diet, though Cieza, in recording his long journey through Ecuador and Peru, often describes the fertility of the land. Moreover, in Inca centres built along the principal roads, massive quantities of foodstuffs were stored; accounts also survive of the great efforts made by the Incas to improve irrigation and thereby increase food production throughout their empire.

CHAPTER EIGHT

THE BOUNDLESS REALM

A Diverse Pattern

In recent years, surviving traces of the Inca presence throughout the length and breadth of their empire have been the object of intense study by archaeologists. Their research reveals a complex infrastructure and suggests a pattern of firm control. Hence the reader might assume that this great domain, stretching from north of the equator to a latitude of 35° south, was basically homogeneous.

But in reality the empire was no monolithic entity, subject to a uniform system of government. Faced with marked variations between different regions, the Inca power structure displayed a notable ability to adapt itself to diverse conditions. Variable factors included the ecology of a given terrain, the culture of its people, and the length of time since it was first conquered. Only in the very broadest terms was the ecological pattern of the empire fairly uniform. Throughout most of its extent the coast was desert or semi-desert, while the hinterland rose steeply to the *altiplano*, surmounted by the snow-capped Andes, before descending more gradually on the eastern side into tropical and sub-tropical plains on the far side of the Cordillera; at an altitude of about 1500 metres the hot and damp environment tended to serve as a barrier to further Inca penetration of the interior.

Accordingly, before describing the basic features of Inca rule and its effect upon subject peoples, a few comments on the varying culture and ecology of the principal regions may be useful.

The Core Region

The Inca themselves were natives of the sierra; the very heartland of their realm lay in the central highlands of present-day Peru. In the last centuries prior to the rise of Cuzco, this extensive region had been split into a number of warlike fiefs, often occupying a single valley, where the larger chiefdoms constantly sought to dominate their smaller neighbours. Once conquered by the Incas, these fiefs were placed under the control of a series of planned administrative centres. The highlands of Ecuador were in many respects a northerly projection of this homeland; as we have seen, the principal city, Tumebamba, almost ranked as a second Cuzco.

Some confusion over Inca rule in Ecuador may arise because many Spanish chroniclers overstress the importance of Quito, which became the Spanish capital. However, an early eyewitness, Cieza de León, who passed through the region in 1548, says little of Quito, but writes of the 'sumptuous palaces' in the vicinity of Tumebamba, of which he saw ruins. He describes the Temple of the Sun as built with huge blocks of stone, reminiscent of the more grandiose Inca buildings in Cuzco and elsewhere. He tells of Inca palaces with straw roofs, but which contained the finest stone sculpture and many gold objects. Numerous goldsmiths were employed in Tumebamba and Cieza mentions large stores formerly filled with quantities of fine woollen textiles, woven by the 200 virgins housed in the Sun Temple. He writes of the Cañaris, the inhabitants of the Tumebamba region, and mentions their long hair, a custom that survives among the people who occupy the verdant countryside that surrounds the present-day city, now called Cuenca.

Quito, in contrast, was probably noted in Inca times more for its strategic location and for its use as a commercial centre. As Frank Solomon points out, the scarce body of testimony about Inca Quito is only slightly enriched by recent archaeological research, which has done little to increase our limited knowledge of Inca buildings in Quito; the remains of military architecture in the form of forts around the city are more striking than any faint traces of ceremonial buildings.

A leading centre in highland Peru, but by no means the largest, was Cajamarca, where the last Inca, Atahualpa, was captured by the

Spaniards; the plaza, which they describe as larger than any in Spain, was surrounded by a high wall and entered by two doorways. Little is left of its late pre-Hispanic ruins and archaeologists have unearthed only one Inca structure.

Whereas such places as Cajamarca and Chan Chan had thrived before the Inca conquest, in other inland valleys the Incas would construct centres that served imperial personnel on a rotating basis; such places in one way or another mirrored certain facets of Cuzco itself. They invariably included such typical features as a plaza, a principal palace, and a Temple of the Sun. Typical of such sites is Incahuasi, situated twenty-eight kilometres inland from the coast in the Río Cañete Valley near Lima. (As we shall later see, the Inca also used certain existing sites in the coastal region as administrative centres.) Incahuasi was excavated in recent years by John Hyslop, who suggests that Cuzco's formal layout was at least partly present, including the integration of some of its more important astronomical sightlines into the city's plan.

Huánuco, some 500 kilometres north-west of Cuzco, is the best preserved of the large Inca provincial centres, and has been intensively studied in recent years by a team headed by Craig Morris. Located at some 3700 metres above sea level, in Huánuco a greater number of the original buildings were preserved because it was abandoned after the Conquest and attempts to build a Spanish city on the Inca site bore few results. It is mostly constructed of rough stone, and only the most important structures display fine masonry. A complete map of the city was made, which includes 4000 streets; of these an extensive sample was excavated as representative of the town as a whole.

Not only residential districts, but large storage areas abound, clearly a major feature of such principal centres. Of these, more than one hundred have been excavated; they contained about 38,000 cubic metres of storage space, much of which was used for food. Their significance is borne out by Ortiz de Zuñiga, who made an official visit in 1562 to Huánuco. His report describes the continued delivery of ample supplies of food to this city in early Spanish times.

Huánuco was apparently built fairly quickly to serve as an administrative centre; many of its inhabitants came from other places and worked there as part of their *mit'a* service, a form of tax imposed by the Incas and discussed in more detail below. Like many Inca centres, it has no defensive military works and no walls. In many such instances the Incas apparently relied less on military occupation than on the prompt transfer of large and reliable *mitimae* groups who served to control newly conquered peoples.

In recent years, archaeologists have paid increasing attention to the manner in which people live today in such climatic conditions. For instance, Ann Kendall has investigated country dwellings in the Valley of Cuzco, a form of research which helps us to understand how people survived so well in a rather inclement environment. Incidentally, guinea pigs, native to Peru, are still reared today in many houses. At altitudes where for much of the year a tropical heat prevails during the day, whereas, say, dried ducks or even potatoes freeze at night, storage becomes a key technique.

The Magic of Machu Picchu

In writing of surviving vestiges of Inca imperial architecture, the most striking, but by no means the largest, is Machu Picchu, now one of the leading tourist attractions of all Latin America. It is impressive both for the sheer beauty of the site and for the perfect integration of architecture and environment. On arriving on the little train, one is almost surprised to learn that Machu Picchu lies at a lower altitude than Cuzco, a fact which accounts for its more lush vegetation.

This awe-inspiring site was discovered by an American, Hiram Bingham, who was searching for the main stronghold of the rebel Inca 'Emperor' Manco. He set out in July of 1911 with two companions for the territory adjacent to the Río Urubamba. After crossing the river, he came suddenly upon a breathtaking sight: a magnificent flight of stone terraces, rising up the steep hillside. Climbing as far as he could through an apparently virgin forest, he discovered building after building buried in the thick undergrowth. To quote Bingham: 'I suddenly found myself in a maze of beautiful granite houses.'

Bingham, some years after his discovery of Machu Picchu, explored the hills above the Río Urubamba, where he found a whole series of Inca sites along what is known as the Inca Trail, inventing appropriate names for those that had no local appellation. These places were cleared in the 1940s in expeditions that also uncovered yet more sites, including Cusichaca, later studied and restored by Ann Kendall; her team even rebuilt certain Inca irrigation channels for use by local farmers.

A visitor to Machu Picchu may be well advised to first climb up to the top part, known as the Upper Cemetery, which is flanked by two defensive walls. This vantage point offers a good view of the group of fine buildings of the inner city, divided by central squares, somewhat reminiscent of the plan of Cuzco itself.

At the end of the Upper Cemetery stands a small construction known as the 'watchman's hut'. The steeply sloping roof has now been restored; for visitors such as myself it provided a happy refuge from a shower of rain.

The inner city itself consists of finely constructed buildings that give the impression of serving as a kind of 'sacred sector'. Stairs at the end of this inner group lead down to the famous *torréon* or bastion, whose curved wall (a rare feature in Inca architecture) somewhat recalls the curved walls of the Sun Temple of Coricancha in Cuzco.

However famous for its stonework, Machu Picchu lacks the dimensions of a true city. Its 200 buildings allow for a population of about 1000 inhabitants. Originally described as a fortress, the massive literature on the site now offers many alternatives as to its possible use, which remains a mystery. A constellation of even smaller sites was found in its vicinity; Winay Wayna, for example, consists of a group of twenty chambers, a series of baths on the hillside, a circular tower and many terraces. In this chain of settlements on the Río Urubamba the presence of elaborate terraces and of sacred architecture suggests a significance that was both ceremonial and agricultural rather than military.

Coastal Peru

The thriving principalities of the south coast of Peru, lying to the west and south-west of Cuzco, were among the earlier objectives of Inca expansion.

In the southernmost valleys of Ica and Nazca, the invaders met with little opposition, but further to the north-west others resisted fiercely.

Typical of the latter was Chincha, among the most important principalities of the southern coast. The conquered Chincha capital became
an Inca provincial centre, complete with its temple to the sun; *mitimaes*
from other places were settled in the vicinity. The Chincha ruler was
accorded a status of high prestige in the imperial hierarchy, and at
conqueror Francisco Pizarro's first encounter with Atahualpa in Cajamarca, this prince was the only other dignitary reported to be borne in
a litter.

Further to the north, in the central sector of the Peruvian coast, two
principalities were predominant, Ychma, which included the Valley of
Lima, and Collique, to the north of present-day Lima. The surviving
sites of Cajamarquilla and Pachacamac were both then situated in
Ychma. The latter had become a major city in the Huari era and its
population probably began to decline before the end of this period.

However, Pachacamac retained its prestige as a shrine; famed for
its sanctity, it attracted pilgrims from places far distant; the captive
Atahualpa's account of the store of golden treasure owned by its idol
enthralled Pizarro. An early Spanish visitor was Francisco de Xerez,
who accompanied Hernando Pizarro, Francisco's brother, on a visit to
Pachacamac, whose ruins can still be visited today and are reasonably
accessible from Lima.

The purpose of Hernando Pizarro was to search for the massive
amount of gold stored at the shrine. The expedition consisted of twenty
horsemen, and Xerez gives a fascinating account of a perhaps typical
journey by groups of Spaniards who foraged for gold in the early days
after their arrival. They set out from Cajamarca on 5 January 1533, and
travelled down the great road that led to Cuzco. After nearly two
weeks, including periods of rest, they branched off the main highway
at Marcara and a few days later reached Pachacamac.

The local *cacique* initially produced only modest quantities of bullion
and declared that he had no more. The Captain, as Xerez calls Hernando
Pizarro, said he would be interested to see the famous idol that served
as an oracle. The idol was so hallowed that people came to consult it
from distances of up to 300 leagues, bringing lavish gifts of gold and
silver; in addition, it received much precious metal from the people of
the surrounding region.

The priests were stunned by the admission of the Captain to the idol's presence and feared that they would all die as a punishment for this desecration. The quest for gold was ultimately satisfied because Xerez relates that many *caciques* from nearby centres, including the important lord of Chincha, came to Pachacamac and brought lavish gifts that were added to the booty taken by the Spanish themselves from the Sun Temple, situated near the oracle.

On the northern part of the Peruvian coast lay the great kingdom of Chimor, described in some detail in Chapter 5. At the time of its conquest by Tupac Inca, it was in no respect a moribund realm, already set on the road to ruin. On the contrary, it was still actively extending its bounds at a time when Inca expansion was gaining momentum.

In marked contrast to copious data on Chimor provided by modern archaeological research, the traditional sources' reports of the Inca conquest are both cursory and contradictory and do scant justice to what must have been one of the most dazzling, if not the most daunting, chapters in the annals of Inca warfare. Certain reports that Chimor yielded without a struggle tend to lack credibility; all accounts concur that the ruler was carried off to Cuzco, and it is surely open to doubt that such a potent monarch would submit to a degrading fate and surrender his imposing capital without a fight.

Chimor was mercilessly looted by the Incas and some of the gold sent to Cuzco was used to make a great band of precious metal extended round the wall of the Temple of the Sun in Coricancha. The vanquished ruler was kept secluded in Cuzco; a son mounted his throne as an Inca puppet, succeeded in turn by his son and grandson, though any pretence of power still exercised by such phantom rulers was methodically eroded. Chimor was conspicuous for its organization and culture, though we still know too little of its government to be sure just what aspects the Incas might have borrowed. The paucity of Inca-style buildings or artefacts located in this region bears witness to a certain respect for Chimu norms and to a consequent reluctance to impose their own culture. By archaeological evidence alone, it would be hard to establish an 'Inca Period' in the area, in contrast to the great constructions and copious amounts of pure Inca pottery present in Pachacamac.

Collasuyu

Of comparable importance to the Inca Empire was Collasuyu, the region adjacent to Lake Titicaca. While the splendours of the Tiahuanaco civilization had long since faded, many tales bear witness to the very close links between Collao and the Inca legendary past. The Valley of Cuzco and the Collao *altiplano* may tend to be regarded as interdependent regions and certain sources even suggest that Aymara-speaking principalities supported Pachacutec against the Chancas.

Notwithstanding any prior links on a basis of virtual equality between Collas and Incas, Pachacutec in the initial phase of Inca long-range expansion imposed his will on the Collas by force, defeating in battle the lord of Hatunqolla and annexing his kingdom. While Hatunqolla thereafter served as an Inca base complete with a temple to the sun and many storehouses, the main provincial centre of the region in Inca times was Chuquito, the capital of the Lupaqa chiefdom, situated a little further to the south-east, near the present-day lakeside city of Puno.

The administration of the region by the Incas' Spanish successors is described in some detail in the official *Visita* of Garci Díez de San Miguel, made in 1567. He describes a populous and prosperous kingdom, still ruled, as in Inca times, by two kings named Cari and Cusi.

Collao's famous shrine, Copacabana, situated on a peninsula at the south end of Lake Titicaca, was first occupied by Tupac Inca, who installed carefully chosen *mitimae* groups to guard the precincts and to supervise the flow of pilgrims. Among other characteristics, the Collas were distinguished by a peculiar form of men's head-dress consisting of a tall, brimless hat which narrowed at the top, depicted in an illustration of Huaman Poma. Colla male heads were deliberately deformed to conform to the shape of this hat, worn in the entire Lake Titicaca region; to achieve this purpose, braided wool was wrapped round an infant's head for more than a year after birth.

In marked contrast to the very high altitudes of the Titicaca region, the lush Bolivian Valley of Cochabamba to the south-east stands at a more temperate level of 2100 metres; also conquered by Tupac, it became under his successor a major imperial bastion. Settled by many *mitimaes* from different provinces, this rich valley was transformed into a veritable breadbasket, providing copious provisions for Inca personnel who served in the southern parts of the empire.

Among the more notable surviving sites of the surrounding region are Incaracay and Incallacta, both of which appear to have combined the dual function of fortress and place of residence. Nordensköld, who investigated the latter site as long ago as 1915, mentions a palace with thick walls, but describes the place mainly as a fortress.

In the more distinct marches of empire south of Cochabamba, remains of larger administrative centres are conspicuous by their absence. While many vestiges of Inca occupation of this region have been unearthed in recent years, it seems that when they settled in local towns they merely adapted them to suit their residential and administrative needs; for instance, nothing in north-western Argentina can remotely be compared with Inca remains in Tumebamba, Ecuador. Since this southern territory had probably only been consolidated in the reign of the last Inca, the time needed for urban development may have been limited. While fine Inca stone masonry is apparently absent in Argentina and Chile, the Argentinian archaeologist Rodolfo Raffino and his colleagues have discovered the remains of a number of forts in southern Bolivia and north-western Argentina; it is hard to say to what extent these were frontier posts. Raffino also mentions forts in Chile near the Río Maule, the probable limit of Inca-controlled territory. Further to the north-west, fairly extensive remains of Inca occupation survive. Hanns Niemayer discovered not only large amounts of Inca shards in the Río Copiapo Valley, but also ample evidence of Inca mining activities. As we have seen, the Incas encountered fierce resistance in Chile, a remote province that was probably only in the earlier stages of pacification.

Imperial Infrastructure

Fundamental to the control of an empire of vast dimensions, embracing such varied and intractable terrain, was infrastructure. In this respect the crowning Inca achievement was their road network, though its fullest extent will never be known, since some roads have physically disappeared. However, many others are still intact, and have been studied in recent times. The Inca Road Project, carried out between 1978 and 1981 under the direction of John Hyslop, ranks among the finest achievements in contemporary Andean studies.

Some roads fall into special categories, such as those leading to high-altitude sanctuaries, usually well above 5000 metres. Other roads were built for military purposes. Most, however, served mainly administrative ends, being used for the transportation of goods. The great coastal highway that crosses the Atacama Desert and connects Cuzco with central Chile belongs to this category; it would have had little military importance because water supplies were too scarce.

Hyslop surveyed a total length of 108 kilometres of the Atacama Desert road, part of which was still in an excellent state of preservation; it appears to have had an original width of three metres. He found in all thirty-two *tampu* staging posts and other sites along the roads.

Of all Inca roads, the most important was the Cuzco–Quito highland route. Many large Inca centres lie on it and no road in the empire was consistently as wide; numerous reports survive since many early Spanish travellers used it, and it is the road most frequently described in historical sources. Any early Spanish visitor to the Andean highlands was likely to travel on this basic highway. The average width, even when crossing agricultural land, is between four and six metres, but part of it is as much as fourteen metres wide. Another important road, often described, is the north coastal road connecting the Río Lambayeque and Moche Valleys, to which Cieza de León devotes several detailed chapters; according to Hyslop, this road was part of a network already built by pre-Inca peoples of the region. Hyslop, in addition, identified and described the road between Santiago de Chile and the Río Aconcagua, situated in the empire's southernmost extreme, so recently conquered.

The road builders faced many problems in dealing with vastly different types of terrain. Coastal arteries built on sandy land needed no artificial surface. Those built over rocky ground required construction only when they climbed steep slopes. Many roads passed through agricultural lands; they were lined by sidewalls used, according to early chroniclers, to protect crops from travellers and animals. The height of these walls was usually one to two metres, thus forming a real rather than a symbolical barrier. Among the most remarkable features of Inca roadways are the elevated causeways, where the bed is raised one-half to two metres above the surface of surrounding water; the most remarkable, described by Spanish chroniclers, were situated in the vicinity of Cuzco. Another major causeway on the shore of Lake Titicaca leads southwards from the important centre of Chucuito for a distance of five kilometres, crossing two shallow bays of the lake; part of the causeway has stone sidewalks.

Bridges were a key feature of the road system. Many of these were fairly simple structures, placed on abutments of stone masonry. But what so impressed the early Spaniards were the suspension bridges with fibre superstructures. These were apparently new to the Europeans and the first crossings on such swaying devices were made with trepidation. Suspension bridges, such as the great bridge over the Río Apurimac, were able to span considerable distances; they could be made of locally available fibres, but suffered from the disadvantage that they needed constant maintenance. Hyslop insists that the hanging bridges of the Incas were much more sophisticated than the few that still exist today; for instance, the sides of one bridge seen by the conquistador Sancho de la Hoz were so carefully crafted that even if a horse fell on all fours, it could not tumble off. Sancho points out that this was done to prevent travellers from falling into the river below, since in regions far from the sea, almost no Indians could swim!

Integral to the road network were the *tampu*, the roadside lodging and storage areas situated at a day's walk apart. One major purpose of the *tampu* was the safekeeping of arms, clothing, fuel and foodstuffs essential to the functioning of the empire.

In contrast to the more solidly built *tampu*, it is harder for archaeologists to identify the *chaski* posts, made of perishable wood and thatch, placed at much shorter intervals than the *tampu* to serve the system of relay runners who passed small objects and messages over great distances in a matter of days. Cieza de León describes them as small houses, occupied by two men drawn from the local population. They were sworn to the strictest secrecy concerning the messages that they bore; in the absence of any form of writing, they perhaps ran the risk of becoming garbled when repeated many times over from one *chaski* to another!

Imperial Government

Information on Inca imperial rule has traditionally been based mainly on accounts by Spanish chroniclers; however, on such aspects as storage facilities, communications, irrigation works and agriculture in general, archaeological research now offers an ever increasing flow of concrete data.

Much information on imperial government at regional levels derives from two early chronicles, that of Damián de la Bandera on the region of Huamanga, written in 1557, and that of Castro-Ortega Morejón on Chincha, written in 1558. Apart from the important details provided by these and other Spanish *Visitas*, Cieza de León and Polo de Ondegardo offer much general data on the role of provincial governors and the system of land distribution.

Such sources concur that each province of the empire was ruled by a governor chosen from the ranks of the Inca elite. They resided in the main provincial centres, where a temple of the sun god symbolized Inca supremacy. In addition to the temples, Cieza mentions the presence in such places of a strong 'garrison', together with silversmiths and other artisans, implicitly formed by loyal *mitimae* groups drawn from another region.

Periodically the reigning monarch would visit a province, where he was regaled by his governor with dazzling pomp and ceremony. Cieza adds that he himself came to know a few provincial governors who had continued to exert a certain authority even after the Spanish Conquest. Many details of the status of such proconsuls remain unknown; for instance, it is hard to determine whether they possessed lands in the provinces that they ruled.

The sources also describe a different class of officials described as visitors, or inspectors, who appeared from time to time and made reports to the central government on specific matters, such as the accuracy of the numerical headcount of population provided by *quipu* knots. Other inspectors were concerned with the administration of justice or the collection of tribute. A special group of visitors was charged with the care of the *mamaconas*, the temple virgins devoted to the cult of the sun.

The previous rulers of the lands conquered by the Incas, usually known as *curacas*, also played an important role. Such *curacas* were of highly disparate standing; the term might include, on the one hand, men who had control over powerful kingdoms, such as those of Collao, which they had ruled since time immemorial, but applied equally to the headman of a small valley, containing three or four villages. Such disparities arose not only from the size of their domain but also from profound cultural differences between the sierra and the coast, between groups of herdsmen in the *altiplano* and communities based on irrigated lands at lower altitudes.

The Inca ruler, or in effect the Inca state, in theory became the owner not only of all land in a newly conquered province, apart from that set aside for the community as a whole; he also took possession of mines and herds of llamas. The *curaca* retained at least the right to labour service from the people of his community and, in fact if not in theory, according to reports from Spanish administrators, was also left in control of a portion of his previous lands. Garcilasco, for instance, writes of *curaca* land ownership and asserts that in each place the people were under an obligation to cultivate these *curaca* holdings. Always anxious to stress the benign nature of Inca rule, the chronicler further states that the poorer people only had the duty to serve the *curaca* after they had tilled their own fields; he claims that during the reign of Huayna Capac an official was put to death because he arranged for the cultivation of the lord's property before that of a poor widow!

The *curacas* had certain administrative functions, including the organization of the *mita*, the universal labour service that provided the goods and services exacted by the Inca state; in addition they played a key role in the exchange of gifts basic to the complex Inca rituals of reciprocity. However, while these local chiefs retained certain powers and privileges, Inca control was strict; sons of provincial lords, or at least those of the more important members of this elite, were obliged to reside at the Inca's court from the age of fourteen; this enabled their masters to form a good idea as to which son would be the more apt successor; in many cases this was not necessarily the eldest.

Other limitations were placed on the *curacas*; while they were forbidden to put their subjects to death, they could flog them in certain instances. Moreover, they had to obey strict rules of protocol. Only a high-ranking prince had the privilege of making a ceremonial toast to the Inca monarch (to whom he would present his cup after drinking). Their resources, moreover, were certainly curtailed in comparison to their revenues in pre-Inca times, when surplus wealth drained off from the population would have been at their entire disposal.

Bonds of Empire

Before considering other aspects of Inca rule, the imperial cult needs to be stressed, as a means of cementing the Inca domain. This cult, centred on Cuzco, served as a model, on a reduced scale, not only of the empire, but of the universe, since the empire, known as Tahuantin-suyu, was conceived as corresponding with the universe itself.

The religious factor served not only as a possible motive for conquest, but also as a means to secure the loyalty of those conquered. The sources stress the widespread imposition of the solar deity, Inti, personified by the ruler himself as the son of the sun.

Not only in Cuzco, but in provincial centres, with their main temple dedicated to the sun, solar worship came to be the dominant religious force, pre-eminent in funeral ceremonies and other principal rites. In contrast, the Incas would reportedly take hostage the main idol of a newly conquered province and send it to Cuzco, where it was honoured with the same rites as in its place of origin. People of that province were brought to Cuzco to ensure the correct observance of the cult of their deity, whose effigy was lodged in the capital. Rites of the local deities continued to be celebrated in each region, but the cult of the sun was imposed upon these local religions as a unifying force.

Imperial cohesion was also furthered by the overall use of the Quechua language, spoken by the Incas, though Aymara was the native tongue of the extensive territory of Collao. The provincial elite were expected to know the language of Cuzco. The importance of Quechua as a lingua franca was further enhanced by the babel of tongues created by the moving of so many groups of migrants from one corner of the empire to another; these *mitimaes* were obliged at times to speak Quechua, while also conserving their own native idiom in their new homes, where some other tongue also prevailed. After the Conquest the Spaniards also furthered the use of Quechua; the Viceroy Francisco de Toledo, convinced that this language would be the best instrument for spreading the Gospel, established chairs in Lima University for the teaching of Quechua, in which the catechism was also printed. The Spaniards even reported that in north-western Argentina some seventy years after the Conquest, Quechua was spoken, though elements of Aymara had also spread to that region.

The Land

As in other pre-industrial societies, for the Incas land ownership was the symbol of both wealth and status.

However, certain surviving accounts of the landholding system throughout the empire tend to reveal discrepancies between theory and practice. On this rather complex problem, Bernabé Cobo gives a useful outline of the data of earlier sources.

In conformity with such reports he asserts that when the Incas first conquered a town or province they would divide the land into three parts; the first for the state religion, the second for the Inca ruler, and the third for the community as a whole. In many places the division between church and state was not equal; in some instances the ruler took the largest share, while in others the greater part of the land belonged to the cult of the sun and other gods. The *curacas* would divide the community holdings among the common people in accordance with the size of each family; if men were absent on military service, others would till their fields.

To some extent the notion that the Inca state disposed of all lands may be regarded as a legal fiction since, as we have seen, the *curacas* also retained certain rights to land, though these are harder to define. In practice the grant by the Inca ruler of land to *curacas* was perhaps nothing more than a confirmation by the state of certain existing rights, deriving from pre-Inca times.

While the Incas thus appropriated many holdings, they not only did much to increase productivity, but also brought extensive additional land into cultivation. Irrigation had existed in Peru for millennia before their time, but both on the coast and in the highlands, archaeological research demonstrates the impressive scale of Inca irrigation works. They not only dammed rivers but even corrected, or turned, their courses. For instance, at Cajamarca a canal was cut in the rock for more than 800 metres and Inca engineers gave it a zigzag course to slow down the flow of water.

In the difficult highland terrain the system of man-made terraces was so extended in Inca times as to give to many Andean valleys the appearance of veritable staircases. The banks were held up by walls of stone, the height of which varied with the steepness of the incline.

Mines and Herds

While the exact proportion of lands which the Inca state expropriated may be open to question, their claim to monopolize the all-important mining rights is more clearly defined. Metallurgy was an ancient craft among the Andean peoples, but the insatiable Inca appetite led to an intensified search for precious metals, extended to distant regions.

The sources stress outright ownership by the Inca ruler of all mines and herds. Possibly the lure of gold was the main motive for the conquest of far-off Chile, where mines are known to have been exploited by the Inca conquerors. Various Inca mining settlements have been also identified by archaeologists in north-west Argentina, where early Spanish colonial sources refer to Inca mines. Collao was rich in minerals, particularly in the area to the north-east of Lake Titicaca. Not only provincial governors but also local *curacas* in many parts of the empire would make presents of gold and silver to the ruler, which implies that these *curacas* also retained an interest in mining activity, if only to enable them to bestow gifts on their sovereign.

Various chroniclers attribute to the Inca the direct ownership of the great herds of cameloids. The domestication of the llama and the alpaca endowed the Peruvian economy with a unique asset among the peoples of the New World, generally ill-provided with domesticated animals.

Originally cameloids flourished mainly in the very high altitudes of Collasuyu, where the local rulers had traditionally possessed large herds. They were prized for their wool, used to make the luxury textiles needed for religious rites; they also played a role in the complex procedure of offering gifts to the elite of Cuzco. The Inca himself consumed on a large scale exquisite textiles made of the wool of cameloids. He seldom wore a garment more than once and would change clothing several times a day; his litter was also covered with the finest material. Many of the special garments reserved for the emperor and his family were woven in the temples by the Virgins of the Sun.

The llama was also important as a beast of burden. An extremely frugal animal, it can go without food or water for several days, but can only carry a load of about twenty-five kilos for a distance of fifteen kilometres per day. It also served in Inca religion as a major sacrificial offering, white llamas being the preferred victims of the sun. Each morning in Cuzco one llama was sacrificed by cutting its throat, while keeping its head turned towards the sun, to which it was being offered. The animal was then burned on a special brazier. Llamas were offered in Bolivia not only to the sun, but to the local thunder god, Illapa.

The Incas, apart from Collao, established herds in many other regions of the *altiplano* where none had existed before. Hence the state herds were very numerous, serving military as well as ceremonial ends. In contrast, the Spanish conquistadors were more interested in the llama as a source of meat!

Social Engineering

Fundamental to Inca control of the empire was the *mitimae* system, involving mass transfers of populations from one region to another. The Incas sought to indoctrinate newly conquered peoples and to instil in them a subservience so absolute that large groups whose loyalty to the Inca system was undoubted would obey the call to abandon their homeland and migrate to a newly conquered territory. Here they would preserve their own rites and customs, and at the same time keep a watchful eye on the local inhabitants, thus furthering the process of absorption, whereby they in turn were also converted into loyal subjects. So strict was the Inca method of control, whether in Cuzco or elsewhere, that no record survives of any resistance to this form of social engineering, which has even been likened to the moving of pieces on a chessboard. The chronicler Bernabé Cobo describes the system as essential to the subjection of new provinces; the migrants were normally settled in the provincial capitals; Cobo adds that when the ruler subjected a province, he would remove up to six or seven thousand families, and replace them with these *mitimaes*.

This policy was vigorously applied, for instance, in distant Ecuador, whose tribes had so fiercely resisted the Incas. In certain regions, large groups of conquered peoples were removed and replaced by settlers from other parts of the empire; in early Colonial times, many of the inhabitants of the Quito region were either Quechua- or Aymara-speaking Indians from Bolivia. Enclaves of southern colonists also served as focal centres of Inca influence in the northern part of Ecuador, where even today some of these imported settlers can be distinguished by the dress and customs of the inhabitants. People from Ecuador in their turn were sent to many other provinces; among the many *mitimae* groups brought by the emperor, Huayna Capac, to the important Inca centre of Cochabamba in Bolivia, were people from the Quito region. To Cochabamba this ruler also transferred groups of silversmiths from coastal Peru, who faced an arduous trek over the Andes to reach their new home. Most *mitimaes* that had been settled in the Lupaqa kingdom, on the shores of Lake Titicaca, probably at a relatively early date, came from the Valley of Cuzco, their original homeland.

Cieza de Léon, who identified many such groups on his long journey southwards, divides the *mitimaes* into three categories. The first served basically military ends, having been sent to establish enclaves, or in effect garrisons, as a protection against savage frontier peoples. *Mitimae* garrisons of this type were also stationed further north along the critical frontier region of the ever rebellious Bracamoros and Chachapoyas, against whom the later emperors conducted many rather fruitless campaigns. The second category, whose function was social as well as military, consisted of contingents sent when a new territory was organized into provinces. Installed not solely for security reasons, they also helped to further the process of Incaization of the local inhabitants. The third type of *mitimaes*, economic rather than military, were those sent to populate mountain valleys within the empire that were fertile, but that lacked people to till the soil.

Labour as Tribute

Throughout the empire, at least in theory, the peasant population served the state by providing labour rather than by paying tribute in kind.

Mit'a was the term generally used for this part-time labour service imposed both in the Cuzco region and in the provinces. The state's recruitment of labour, in addition to the paramount obligation of military service, was not limited to the tilling of the lands of the ruling class; the weaving of textiles and the making of tools were also important. Apart from such tasks, and from the massive demand of military manpower, the need for labour for building temples and palaces, both in Cuzco and elsewhere, for road making, for work on fortresses, irrigation and mining projects, as well as for conveying goods and materials from one place to another assumed formidable proportions. The demand for labour for transportation of goods alone must have been colossal; for instance, the emperor Huayna Capac ordered that plentiful supplies of timber for making rafts should be carried all the way from the coast of Ecuador to the shore of Lake Titicaca, about 1500 kilometres distant.

A notable aspect of the organization of *mit'a* manpower is the reported use of a decimal system, not only for military but for civil purposes, as a means of apportioning the work required in each area. Many sources concur that the peasants were divided into bodies of 10,000 who would be placed under the control of a leading *curaca*. These would be in turn subdivided into 10 contingents of 1000, and thereafter into groups of 100 or even smaller, each administered by lesser officials.

In practice, obvious doubts arise as to just how a village population could be made to conform to such a precise decimal system; none the less, a preference for this numerical arrangement might account for a tendency to adjust the boundaries of communities in order to attain some degree of uniformity.

At least some version of a decimal system could more readily be applied to military service. The numbers thus recruited through the *mit'a* are hard to quantify, but given the ever greater distances involved in waging imperial wars, the obligation clearly became increasingly burdensome. The very nature of the *mit'a* suggests that this form of recruitment did not involve full-time military service. Even if this *mit'a* service was the prime obligation of many males, just as the weaving of cloth was the work of females, the soldiers surely had to return to their villages for part of the year, since women and old men could hardly be expected to cultivate not only their own communal holdings, but also the state lands and those of the *curacas*.

The services rendered by the *mit'a* system were to some extent reinforced by full-time labourers known as *yanaconas*, or *yanas*. Information as to their origins, numbers and precise status is far from complete. John Murra, who has written extensively on this subject, states that he simply does not know whether they can truly be described as slaves. The *yanas*, who had apparently been torn as individuals from their original houses, were entirely dependent on those for whom they worked, often as domestic servants, bodyguards or litter bearers. Certain *yanas* even attained a privileged status, being given other *yanas* as servants, while some also received women as a reward for their zeal in working for their Inca masters.

The Spanish chroniclers tend to stress the notion that throughout the empire the common people contributed to the state and to its elite services rather than goods. But if the obligation of the labourer supposedly took the form of service, what provincial governors and *curacas* actually received were the goods that he made, particularly in the case of artisans and other specialists. The cornucopia of luxury articles produced by such craftsmen amazed the Spaniards, who found them both in Cuzco and in the provinces.

Craig Morris in his archaeological study of Inca warehousing describes facilities of enormous size and sophistication. While records of storage for the most part perished with the last interpreters of *quipu* knots, the storehouses themselves still dot the hills above the ruins of many Inca towns.

A large part of the fine cloth and other goods that conferred status was naturally sent to the capital, where so many of the elite recipients resided. The accumulation of exquisite adornments stored in Cuzco, which so astonished the first Spaniards, appeared to have far exceeded even the extravagant needs of the upper social strata.

One reason for this accumulation of so much finery in Cuzco itself was that if later sent to other provinces as gifts, these in theory came from Cuzco; the prestige of such gifts was enhanced by association with the ruler and his capital. In contrast, ordinary subsistence items were more often taken not to Cuzco but to big provincial centres such as Huánuco. None the less, the huge amounts of luxury cloth that the Spaniards saw in Cajamarca were probably the result of the sovereign's temporary presence rather than a sample of Cajamarca's usual supplies.

In the final analysis the whole system may be viewed as a form of redistribution, but one that ministered more to the comforts of the ruling class than to the needs of their humbler subjects. It must, moreover, be borne in mind that as part of the tributary system the common people provided not only for the Inca conquerors, but for their own *curacas*. As such the system surely had ancient roots.

Trade and Barter

While the flow of riches to Cuzco and to provincial storehouses was impressive, interchange of merchandise in the form of trade rather than tribute was more restricted.

In an empire in which climatic variations were so marked, particularly between the *altiplano* and the coast, it might be logical to expect a copious flow of goods from one province to another, managed by well-established merchants. However, the Incas seem to have been strongly averse to the creation of a powerful merchant class and to the creation of a market network in which goods native to different regions might be freely traded. In contrast, they tended to favour a system whereby each region attained a degree of self-sufficiency without too much reliance on its neighbours. Fundamental to this system is what John Murra has described as the principle of 'verticality', whereby polities of the sierra established their own settlements at lower or warmer levels, on or near the coast, and also at higher altitudes than their homeland. Such centrally controlled settlements formed part of what Murra has defined as vertical archipelagos, able to provide produce native to a wide range of ecologies, without recourse to formal trade with other provinces.

A striking example of this system is the Lupaqa kingdom, documented by the *Visita* of Garci Díez de San Miguel in 1567. The Lupaqa, who lived at an altitude of 3600 metres in the vicinity of Lake Titicaca, controlled their own settlement on the coast, situated on the present-day border between Chile and Peru, and also others extending as far as Moquegua, some 160 kilometres to the north-west. Hence they not only were self-sufficient in maize and cotton, but also obtained a whole variety of marine produce.

This system was greatly expanded in the final period of Inca rule and the long-distance operations of the last emperors led to the establishment of settlements up to sixty days' walk from their homeland, suggesting that the vertical archipelago was undergoing fundamental change in the decades immediately before 1532.

Murra's hypothesis ranks as a major contribution to Andean social studies and he himself has been the first to concede that the system had its limitations. Possibly conditions in certain parts of the Andes favoured this approach, whereas elsewhere this was not the case. Certain kingdoms on the shores of Lake Titicaca only established 'islands' towards the Pacific coast, while others made settlements on the edge of the tropical forest on the eastern slopes of the Andes, and had none on the coast.

A preference for regional self-sufficiency also served to stimulate the production of the core provinces, in order to supply the needs of their inhabitants and to satisfy the tributary demands of the Inca state, both for the capital and for other important centres. In this respect much was achieved by the Incas' intensive development of irrigation. This drive to increase agricultural production was gaining momentum at the time of the Conquest; if the Incas invented few new techniques, their use of established skills achieved impressive results. One may recall Huayna Capac's development of the Cochabamba Valley, involving the introduction of large groups of *mitimaes*. Cieza de Léon, in writing of the *mitimae* system, records that it served to populate barren areas, to such an extent that in Inca times very little usable terrain remained uncultivated; the chronicler sadly remarks that whereas the idolatrous Incas cared so much for their lands, the Christian Spaniards were basically destructive.

But while the Incas thus displayed a marked preference for regional self-sufficiency, such a policy clearly did not lead to an absolute ban on trade and barter, though no evidence survives of the use of any form of currency for this purpose.

Some interchange undoubtedly did take place between the empire as a whole and the wilder tribes beyond its boundaries, consisting basically of coca and other tropical products. Cinnamon and coca and other luxuries were shipped northwards to Ecuadorian highland centres. Further to the south, while the Incas seldom sought to conquer warm lands below an altitude of, say, 1500 metres on the reverse slopes of the Andes, a certain interchange of goods, such as honey and wax, took place, together with limited amounts of coca.

Particularly in the more recently conquered northern lands certain forms of trade continued to flourish, both by sea and from places further inland towards Amazonia. Spanish accounts of such activities are few; however, the conquistador Sámano-Xerez records the description, given to him by Francisco Pizarro's pilot, of a great raft sighted off the coast of Ecuador. It had a large cabin and cotton sails, and carried an impressive cargo composed of merchandise of a strictly ceremonial nature that included not only shells, but luxury textiles, together with gold and silver ornaments. The chronicler Zárate also describes native crafts, and was surprised to see a whole fleet of sailing rafts in the vicinity of the island of Puná; some, when used by Spaniards, could carry as many as fifty men and three horses.

Evidence also survives of the activities of merchants who traded the produce of the southern coast of Peru. María Rostworowski cites Colonial documents that write of no less than 6000 merchants who would travel from the Chincha coastal region to Cuzco and Collao; they also went to Ecuador in search of gold and emeralds. (Part of the Pacific shoreline of Ecuador is still known as the Emerald Coast.) These merchants devised a kind of local currency in the form of small pieces of copper, and they had even established a fixed rate of exchange between the value of a given weight of gold and silver.

Regardless of any Inca preference for state systems of interchange, as opposed to private trade, certain tropical or semi-tropical commodities were unquestionably obtained, on an ostensibly private basis, from beyond the imperial boundaries. Tolerance of any survival of traditional trade and barter in the conquered regions of Ecuador might also be due to the abundance of certain ritual items in the unconquered parts of that region. Supreme importance was attached to the *mullu* shells (*Spondylus pictorum*) available in the warmer Ecuadorian waters, but not in the colder sea to the south. Since the Incas did not dominate coastal

Ecuador, any state-controlled mechanism could hardly have satisfied their insatiable demand for spondylus shells for ritual use. These shells were sent not only to the heartland of the empire, but also have now been found as far afield as north-western Argentina and Chile.

An Ecological Mosaic

The Inca Empire, as described above, formed a mosaic of differing ecologies, languages and traditions, on which any theoretical model could only be imposed with a certain flexibility. It was almost impossible for the Inca conquerors to apply identical forms of control upon petty highland chiefdoms and upon the large and long-established Aymara principalities of Collao, let alone upon the great kingdom of Chimor. If in theory the Inca ruler was the supreme lord, and if he and his gods owned almost everything except the peasants' holdings, in practice many concessions were made to established interests. Certain local traditions were respected, and where these were so deep-rooted as, for instance, on the southern coast of Peru, the imprint of Inca culture was more limited than in certain parts of the *altiplano*.

On the one hand, supreme power in each province was wielded by the Inca governor, an *orejón* of the highest standing. The spiritual symbol of this imperial presence was the temple to Inti, the sun. But also basic to the machinery of government were the *curacas*, permitted to retain part of their previous wealth and power, though subject to strict Inca control. The common people were also required to devote much of their time to the service of the state, whether to till the fields or to serve in the army, often in arduous campaigns in far-off lands.

To satisfy the Inca preference for self-sufficiency, each region became in effect a state within a state, supplying most of its own needs, an aim that was reinforced by the settling of large *mitimae* groups from different regions, both to supplement the local labour force, and to ensure its loyalty, and where necessary to provide specialized craftsmen.

It may be true, as many authors maintain, that the presence of merchants and of trade were alien to the Inca spirit. But notwithstanding any predilection for state-controlled interchange, a certain flexibility in practice prevailed, if one is to accept the reports of the existence of thousands of Chincha travelling merchants. The presence of traders in Ecuador is also evident, and probably would have continued in order to obtain both the greatly prized spondylus shells from the coast and tropical produce from the Amazonic lands beyond the Andes.

CHAPTER NINE

THE CONQUEST

Kingdom Divided

It now remains to describe briefly the final episodes in the story of Inca-dominated Peru. Atahualpa's victory in the civil war was dramatic, but his triumph was fleeting. His lugubrious fate, together with that of the Mexican Moctezuma, has been dramatized in novels, dramas, operas and even motion pictures.

However decisive Atahualpa's victory against Huascar, the Inca realm at the time of the Spanish Conquest remained a divided kingdom, in which no final reconciliation had been achieved between the main factions. Surviving accounts, as we have seen, stress the gruesome ferocity of the civil war.

The chronicler Juán de Betanzos is unsparing in his criticism of Huascar, whom he portrays as licentious and cruel. But he is scarcely more flattering when writing of Atahualpa, his own father-in-law, whose atrocities he also describes in detail. As a sample, perhaps apocryphal, of such savagery, he records that on Atahualpa's orders from the living bodies of three Cañari chiefs the hearts were cut out, chopped into very small pieces and eaten by their attendants.

The victor's vengeance was pitiless. Due to certain special ties that linked Huascar and his grandfather, Tupac Inca, not only were the men and women of their ruler's *panaca* slaughtered, but Tupac's own mummy was burned to cinders, an act of sacrilege so horrific as to be unthinkable in more settled times. The forces of Atahualpa even pillaged the shrines of the holy city of Cuzco.

Huascar's rival, Atahualpa, was the confirmed favourite of the armies of the north, previously led by Huayna Capac. Steeled by the rigours of endless campaigning against savage opponents, this force had proved to be the strongest in the empire. However, after its decisive triumph, little attempt was made to seek reconciliation with the defeated supporters of Huascar, who had certainly enjoyed wide support not only in Cuzco, but in many parts of the empire.

The story of the civil war tends to shed a new light on the almost Byzantine complexity of the process whereby potential heirs to the throne came to the fore. While Huascar was also linked to Hanan (upper) Cuzco, which since the time of Pachacutec had tended to be the predominant moiety, the sources suggest that his main allegiance was to the traditional establishment of Hurin (lower) Cuzco. Hence the elevation of Huascar to the throne might be viewed as a kind of counter-revolution on behalf of the conservative religious hierarchy of Hurin against the Hanan military establishment, and in particular against Huayna Capac's northern army.

Such loyalties need to be considered in weighing the true situation in the Inca realm at the time of its destruction. Certain accounts might imply that the more traditional forces of Hurin were in effect subject to the reformist Hanan regime, deriving from the great Pachacutec. But the ascendency of the military coterie of Tumebamba, a city now enjoying the status of a rival 'Centre of the World', created a grave situation for the Cuzcan religious hierarchy and the outbreak of civil war might have fostered in its leaders a mystico-religious urge to restore their ascendency.

Cajamarca

However total Atahualpa's triumph, it was short-lived. At the very moment when he was celebrating the capture of his rival, Huascar, he received ominous tidings of the approach of a small band of beings so strange that they might have come from outer space. Francisco Pizarro had landed at the head of a contingent, exiguous by Inca standards, of 62 horsemen and 106 foot soldiers. Having first captured the island of Puná, he crossed the Gulf of Guayaquil and stormed the city of Tumbez in a night attack.

On 24 September 1532, this minute but intrepid force set forth into the interior; though they were still in territory not fully incorporated into the Inca Empire, the civil war had left its mark upon its inhabitants; towns were in ruins and from the trees hung many bodies of defiant Indians, loyal to Huascar.

Pizarro was by now no stranger to the coast of Ecuador. After a preliminary exploration in 1524 and a second voyage some three years later, which made few discoveries but suffered heavy casualties, he again set sail from Seville in 1530; after a wearisome march along the coast of Ecuador, he had eventually reached Puná.

By a most extraordinary coincidence, Atahualpa and his forces were camped near Cajamarca, which happened to lie directly on Pizarro's line of march. The story of what followed may be briefly summarized in this context. In his detailed narrative of these events, John Hemming offers fascinating details of the bizarre and tragic clash between these two different worlds.

Pizarro duly reached Cajamarca. One of the first buildings which he encountered was a sun temple, complete with a whole series of structures housing the *mamaconas*, or holy women. An eyewitness, Diego de Trujillo, relates that 500 of these temple virgins were paraded in the main square of Cajamarca; to the indignation of an envoy of Atahualpa who had already arrived on the scene, many were now offered to the Spaniards.

The Spanish leader, anxious to proceed formally, then sent his brother, Hernando Pizarro, and Hernando de Soto to visit Atahualpa, accompanied by an Indian known as Martín, an interpreter acquired on Pizarro's previous voyage. A paved road ran for a few miles to the Inca's headquarters, where he had established himself near a sulphur spring beside which were some fairly small buildings where he resided.

The first two Europeans ever to see the Inca were somewhat unnerved by the humiliation of being denied even the mere privilege of beholding his countenance. Two women had stretched a cloth in front of the ruler, through which he could see without being seen himself, 'according to the custom of these lords, who rarely allowed their vassals to look upon them.' Notwithstanding de Soto's request that the cloth be lowered, the Inca merely bent low his head and communicated with him by means of a herald.

Atahualpa even remained impervious when de Soto reared his horse so close that froth from its mouth soiled the ruler's clothes. Some of his guards, who had flinched at the sight of the outlandish beast, were promptly executed, together with all their families. At the end of the interview, *chicha* was served in two gold cups, one of which the Inca drained himself, while the other was offered to Hernando Pizarro; fearing poison, he drank with hesitation. The same ritual was performed with de Soto, but with silver cups. Finally, Atahualpa promised to visit Cajamarca the following day.

The Spaniards were by now becoming conscious of the power and sophistication of the empire that they had encountered. Isolated from the sea by a long march, they were now in the midst of a force which de Soto and Pizarro estimated at 40,000!

Notwithstanding their own military experience and skill, and the superiority of their weapons, the invaders had marched into an impasse. They were no doubt mindful of the tactic that had succeeded so well in Mexico, the kidnapping of the ruler, though confronted with such odds it would have been easier for the Inca to capture Pizarro! It was, therefore, agreed that the latter should decide on the spur of the moment on the best course of action, once Atahualpa had arrived in Cajamarca. The city was ideally suited to the Spaniards' tentative plan: long, low buildings occupied three sides of the main square, and in these Pizarro was able to station his cavalry in three contingents of fifteen to twenty men.

In contrast, Atahualpa had rather light-heartedly devised his visit to the exotic strangers as a kind of ceremonial pageant. He went accompanied by a large escort, according to many sources unarmed except for small battle axes and slings concealed beneath their tunics.

Miguel de Estete offers an eyewitness view by one of the first Europeans to see Atahualpa, and amply confirms the chroniclers' many accounts of the pomp and ceremony that surrounded his movements: 'In a very fine litter with the ends of its timbers covered in silver, came the figure of Atahualpa. Eighty lords carried him on their shoulders, all wearing a rich blue livery. His own person was elaborately adorned with his crown on his head and a collar of large emeralds round his neck. He was seated on the litter, on a small stool with a rich saddle cushion. He stopped when he reached the middle of the square [of Cajamarca] with his body half exposed. The litter was lined with parrot feathers of many colours and embellished with plates of gold and silver.

Behind it came two other litters and two hammocks in which other leading persons travelled. Then came many men in squadrons with head-dresses of gold and silver.'

When he reached Cajamarca, Atahualpa was most surprised to find not a single Spaniard; eventually the Dominican friar Vicente de Valverde emerged, accompanied by the interpreter, Martín. According to most accounts, the Spaniard offered Atahualpa a breviary, which he briefly examined and then threw angrily to the ground. Upon this Pizarro launched his ambush, and his cavalry charged into the mass of the emperor's lightly armed followers. Some resisted, but the mounted Spaniards managed to seize and overturn the royal litter, whose occupant was thus captured. The Spanish cavalry then charged out into the plain and a carnage followed, in the course of which several thousand Indians perished.

The story of what ensued has been told so often that it may be briefly summarized in this context. The following day the Inca tried to extricate himself from his dire predicament by the offer of his famous ransom of a room, seven metres long and five metres wide, to be filled with gold objects. Pizarro duly drew up a document that guaranteed Atahualpa's freedom if the gold was provided within a specified time. In compliance with this agreement, Quizquiz, the Inca's commander in Cuzco, received the order to strip the sacred buildings of all immediately portable gold objects and to dispatch these by special carriers to Cajamarca.

Meanwhile, gold was gradually amassed and taken to Cuzco from other parts of the empire for transportation to Cajamarca. Atahualpa appears to have suffered from a naïve illusion that the Spaniards would honour their promise to release him in return for gold, even to the point of assuming that after setting him free they would simply pack up their spoils and depart for ever. To expedite the completion of the contract, three conquistadors were sent to Cuzco; since no Indian would help them in this task, they themselves prised off 700 plates of gold that shielded the great Temple of the Sun, Coricancha, using copper crowbars. Among other precious objects, a great golden fountain that weighed over 12,000 pesos was dismantled and sent to Cajamarca.

By this time the Spaniards had accumulated a massive hoard of gold and on 16 March 1533, before even waiting for the treasure house to be filled, Pizarro ordered the process of melting down the precious metal to begin. A total of eleven tons was cast into the furnaces, including many exquisite objects, the masterpieces of the Inca goldsmiths. This produced a quota for each horseman of forty kilos of gold, while foot soldiers received half this amount.

The Spaniards meanwhile were fascinated by the elaborate rituals of the captive Inca's daily life, and by the impeccable service that he continued to receive from his retinue. An eyewitness, Francisco de Xerez, relates that he was still held in awe by his subjects; *caciques* would come from far and wide to pay respects to their captive ruler, kissing his feet and hands; he would receive them impassively, not even deigning to look them in the face. Pizarro also treated him with the utmost respect and offered the services of a Dominican padre to instruct him in the Christian faith, as a means to achieving the salvation of his soul.

When Atahualpa saw the relentless melting down of the accumulated treasure, his illusions vanished and he began to despair of previous hopes that his captors would fulfil their pledge to release him. Rumours then began to circulate among the Spaniards that Atahualpa was attempting to mobilize his northern armies, stationed in Ecuador under the command of Rumiñavi, in order that they might mount an expedition and liberate their master.

Such reports, though vigorously denied by the Inca, greatly incensed the Spaniards. The latter were deeply divided as to whether the ruler should promptly be executed as a traitor to their cause. Some had grown fond of the captive, while others viewed him as a constant threat to their own safety. The method of deciding the issue was wholly capricious. During a game of cards, a Nicaraguan Indian appeared who swore that he had seen a vast horde of native troops advancing upon Cajamarca. The governor, Pizarro, was thereby induced against his will to order the immediate death of Atahualpa. There had been no trial and Pizarro merely succumbed to the demands of his own captain, Diego de Almagro, and the royal officials.

The end was pitiless. As night was falling on 26 July 1533, Atahualpa was led into the middle of the square and tied to a stake. Pressed by the Friar Valverde, he requested baptism; as a consequence, instead of being burned alive, he was garrotted by a piece of rope.

Atahualpa was formally buried as a Christian in Cajamarca. Thereafter, however, a native force descended on the city, exhumed the Inca's

Figure 31   Atahualpa with Spanish Guard (illustration by Huaman Poma)

body and transported it for reburial in Quito, at that time controlled by Rumiñavi.

The Conquest

By killing Atahualpa, in Indian eyes the Spaniards had cast themselves in the role of champions of Huascar and as such enjoyed a degree of support among certain elements of the population. However, not only Ecuador, but also much of central Peru was controlled by Atahualpa's northern armies, commanded by his general, Quizquiz. Huascar himself had been killed by his own guards on the orders of Atahualpa, when the latter was already a Spanish captive.

Their southward march was facilitated by the splendid highways built by the Incas. The Spaniards fought no fewer than four battles against these armies; after the final conclusive encounter in the mountains above Cuzco, the forces of Quito simply lost heart and vanished. When they first beheld Cuzco, the triumphant conquistadors described the buildings of the Inca capital, as they had previously done in Mexico, as of greater splendour than anything they had ever seen in Spain.

The occupation of the outer marches of the empire presented fewer problems. In July 1535, Diego de Almagro left Cuzco for Chile at the head of a well-equipped force, supported by great trains of porters, together with 12,000 Indians under the command of Paullu, a son of Huayna Capac. The march through Collao and Charcas met with scant resistance, since both provinces acknowledged the authority of Paullu, as an heir to Huayna Capac. In Chile there was some opposition, and isolated groups of Spaniards were ambushed and killed. Other forces fled to the extreme south, where Indian resistance even outlived Spanish Colonial rule and was only later crushed by the forces of the Chilean Republic in the nineteenth century!

While the Spanish invaders were thus already in control of much of the central and southern part of the empire, the northern Inca forces still held out in Ecuador, now ruled with an iron hand by Rumiñavi, acting more as an independent *condottiere* than a loyal servant of the dead ruler and his heirs. During his master's captivity, Rumiñavi held the ruler's sons and many of his womenfolk in custody. Atahualpa had sent his brother in an attempt to rescue his children, but the prince was murdered by Rumiñavi, flayed and his skin made into a drum.

The Spaniards' attention was naturally drawn to this northern stronghold and its ruthless tyrant. Sebastián de Benalcázar set out from the coast; John Hemming in his account of the Conquest describes what followed as the finest hour of the Inca resistance. Benalcázar occupied Tumebamba, where 3000 Cañaris, still loyal to the cause of Huascar, joined his forces. The Spanish general continued his northern march, and at Teocajas, situated near a mountain pass at an altitude of 4250 metres, was fought the greatest pitched battle of the Conquest; in this encounter, though the Inca force failed to stem the Spanish horsemen, the latter achieved no decisive victory. The Spaniards continued to fight bands of Indians until they eventually reached Quito; finding that all the men had left to join the Inca forces, Benalcázar retaliated by slaughtering their women and children.

Meanwhile, other contenders unexpectedly entered the fray. The famous conquistador of Mexico, Pedro de Alvarado, proceeding from Guatemala, landed on the coast of Ecuador in February 1536. Unfamiliar with the harsh conditions of the Andes, his expedition achieved little; many of his own men and horses froze to death as he tried to penetrate the Cordillera and took the wrong route. On the other hand, Quizquiz, who had fought against the Spaniards in central Peru, returned to Ecuador. But he failed to join forces with Rumiñavi; after both generals had been defeated and killed, the Ecuadorian resistance gradually subsided.

Inca Puppets

Meanwhile, the Spaniards faced different problems in Cuzco itself. Their efforts to install a series of phantom Inca rulers constitutes a bizarre page in Colonial history. The first attempt proved to be short-lived; soon after Atahualpa's burial as a Christian, Huascar's younger brother, Tupac Huallpa, was crowned as Inca in Cajamarca. The traditional ceremonies were scrupulously observed, beginning with a three-day feast of the new ruler in a specially constructed shrine, and ending with his donning the traditional royal fringe, as his followers turned their faces towards the sun. But his reign came to a most untimely end; the new Inca died a few months later in October 1533. The Spaniards, dismayed by their loss, believed that Tupac had been poisoned.

However, undaunted by this setback, they persisted in their attempt to maintain the fiction of Inca rule, and zealously sought a new champion. On entering Cuzco in November 1533, they were greeted by Manco, yet another son of Huayna Capac, who outwardly feigned a servile devotion to Spanish rule. Manco was thus duly crowned as heir to his half-brother, an event marked by precisely the same ritual performed for his predecessor.

Miguel de Estete gives a vivid account of this ceremony, at which European eyewitnesses could observe so many details of the traditional Inca rituals, including the presence of the mummies of the former kings, seated on thrones.

'Such a vast number of people assembled every day that they could only crowd into the square with great difficulty. Manco had all the dead ancestors brought to the festivities. After he had gone with a great entourage to the temple to make an oration to the sun, throughout the morning he proceeded in rotation to the tombs where each [dead Inca] was embalmed. They were then removed with great veneration and reverence, and brought into the city seated on their thrones in order of precedence. There was a litter for each one, with men in its livery to carry it. The natives came down in this way, singing many ballads and giving thanks to the sun . . . They reached the square accompanied by innumerable people and carrying the Inca at their head in his litter. His father, Huayna Capac, was level with him, and the rest similarly in their litters, embalmed and with diadems on their heads. A pavilion had been erected for each of them, and the dead [kings] were placed in these in order, seated on their thrones and surrounded by pages and women with fly whisks in their hands, who ministered to them with as much respect as if they had been alive. Beside each was a reliquary or small altar with his insignia, on which were the fingernails, hair, teeth and other things that had been cut from his limbs after he had been a prince . . . They remained there from eight in the morning until nightfall with no lull in the festivities . . .'

The Spaniards at this stage in their conquest, as a result of stout resistance, suffered from a sense of insecurity that made them reluctant to suppress forthwith all those heathen rituals, so alien to their own faith. Manco was consequently allowed to practise certain traditional ceremonies, almost as if nothing had occurred. For instance, in 1535 Cristóbal de Molina witnessed the celebration of the feast of Inti Raymi, the hallowed rites dedicated to the harvesting of the maize. On this occasion the royal mortuary bundles were again paraded, seated under feather awnings. They were attended by nobles, traditionally attired, with medallions of fine gold on their heels. The rulers' effigies were accompanied by many females, who used fans made of swans' feathers to keep away the flies.

The Great Rebellion

Manco, however, proved to be a most inauspicious choice from the point of view of the Spaniards, for whom he had some startling surprises in store. He managed to flee from Cuzco, was recaptured, but escaped again on the eve of Easter 1536. His second departure from Cuzco heralded the beginning of the great Inca rebellion. The whole valley was soon thronged with Indian troops, as a veritable steamroller of warriors closed in from all sides. The Spaniards ensconced within Cuzco were staggered by the sheer weight of their opponent's forces, estimated by eyewitnesses as numbering between one and two hundred thousand. In contrast to this horde, those besieged within the capital numbered 190, of whom only 80 were mounted.

On 6 May 1536, Manco's force launched its main attack on this exiguous band. They even devised new tactics, unknown in previous Inca campaigns, by arming their slings with red-hot stones wrapped in cotton that would set fire to the thatched roofs. This weapon incidentally completed the ruin of the sacred city, already stripped of its treasures for Atahualpa's ransom, and then looted by the Spaniards before being incinerated by its own people.

The besieged were eventually cornered in a few buildings at the eastern end of the main square. The attackers developed yet another device, the *bola*, consisting of three stones tied to the end of lengths of llama tendons. But despite their ingenuity, they never developed a weapon that could kill, rather than merely harass, a mounted, armoured horseman. The beleaguered Spaniards eventually resolved that their only hope of salvation lay in the recapture of the fortress of Sacsahuaman, the base from which the brunt of the Indian attacks was launched.

A two-day struggle ensued in which Francisco Pizarro's younger brother, Juán, was killed. Finally, the tiny Spanish force, using scaling ladders in a night assault, succeeded in taking the terrace walls of the fortress. Two further days of bitter fighting ensued, after which the

Indian forces took refuge in the two tall towers; when the Spaniards finally overcame their resistance, they put the defenders, 1500 in all, to the sword.

The fall of Sacsahuaman was by no means the end of the siege, which lasted for a further three months, from May to August. Fighting continued throughout this period, apart from a lull at each new moon, when Indian attacks ceased for the celebration of religious rites. In August the pressure on the defenders gradually slackened after Gonzalo Pizarro made a sortie and captured 200 Indians. Their right hands were cut off in the middle of the square and they were then released, thus serving as a grim warning to the besiegers.

Part of the vast Indian horde still concentrated in the hills around Cuzco began to drift away to sow their crops, and the pressure on the Spaniards in the capital eased. In the meantime, however, Manco had entrusted his general, Quizo Yupanqui, with the reconquest of the central highlands of Peru. After a number of victories against isolated groups of Spanish, Quizo was eventually ordered to descend upon Francisco Pizarro's new capital, Lima, and destroy it. Following a six-day investment of the city, Quizo launched a full-scale attack, but once more the Spanish cavalry prevailed, and Quizo was slain, together with many of his commanders.

Manco had meanwhile himself left Cuzco, still besieged by his forces, and moved to Ollantaytambo, some fifty kilometres downstream on the Río Yucay, a great stronghold, part of whose fine Inca masonry still stands almost intact.

The siege of Cuzco was eventually abandoned after Manco learned of the unexpected arrival of the forces of Diego de Almagro, returning from a triumphant campaign in which he had been ably supported by Paullu, Manco's half-brother, an excellent soldier and a fervent supporter of the Spanish cause. Paullu was very popular and it was known that Almagro had encouraged him to claim the Inca crown for himself. Manco, learning that the allegiance owed to him by the surviving Inca forces might pass to Paullu, tried to negotiate with Amalgro but his overtures were rejected.

Manco eventually abandoned Ollantaytambo and took refuge in the remote province of Vilcabamba, which he ruled as a kind of rump empire. He had managed to mount a second, more extensive rebellion, involving hostilities in the distant Charcas region, beyond Lake Titicaca, which finally ended with the Spanish victory at the battle of Cocha-bamba, while other hostilities occurred in the province of Huánuco to the north of Cuzco.

Manco was eventually murdered in 1545, killed by renegade Spaniards who had fled to his mountain stronghold to escape Spanish justice; the assassins were apprehended by the Incas and tortured to death. Probably by this time the Inca army had been reduced to a few thousand soldiers.

Manco's rump empire survived for several decades, successively ruled in its remote fastness by the sons of Manco, until the last emperor, Tupac Amaru, finally succumbed to forces sent by the Viceroy de Toledo in 1572. There was little opposition; an expedition was sent to the Vilcabamba region; the Indians failed to defend the passes giving access to their territory and the Spaniards had no difficulty in breaking the last Inca resistance. Tupac Amaru and a pathetic band of refugees took to the jungle where they were soon captured. His two leading captains were tortured and executed; others, less guilty in the eyes of the Spaniards, had only their right hands severed.

De Toledo had reached the firm conclusion that these last vestiges of the Inca Empire must now be eliminated and he determined to execute the surviving emperor, Tupac Amaru. After a mock trial he was sentenced to death. Huge crowds of weeping Indians lined the streets as the last ruler was led to his execution by decapitation. According to the chronicler Martín de Murua: 'As the multitude of Indians, who completely filled the square, saw that lamentable spectacle and knew that their lord was to die there, they deafened the skies, making them reverberate with their cries and wailing.' The Inca then made a most moving final address, in which he asked everyone to forgive him; he told the Viceroy and the magistrate that he would pray to God for them. The body of Tupac Amaru was interred in the high chapel of the cathedral, the services being performed by the chapter. His head, however, was impaled on the point of a lance; reportedly it became more beautiful every day and at night the Indians would come and adore it, until the Viceroy was informed of this and the head was then buried with the body in the cathedral chapel.

The process of ending this prolonged, if localized, period of Inca resistance had taken place against the rather bizarre background of an embittered struggle between several Spanish factions. The conquistadors, far from being united in their determination to crush the rump empire of Manco, were themselves in a state of all-out civil war, amounting to a virtual rebellion against the King of Spain.

Initially Almagro's triumphant forces, having returned from Chile and saved the beleaguered defenders of Cuzco, occupied the centre of Peru, while those of the three Pizarro brothers, Francisco, Hernando and Gonzalo, virtually controlled Lima and the coast. Hernando Pizarro proceeded to invade central Peru and reached Cuzco, where in 1538 he won a complete victory over Almagro's forces, arrested their leader and had him garrotted.

Following this, the defeated Almagrists rallied under their leader's son, also called Diego; a group of twenty forced their way into Francisco Pizarro's apparently unguarded palace in Lima and killed its occupant. With the death of Francisco, the undisputed leader of the Conquest, the whole enterprise entered a new phase, beginning with the dispatch by Charles V of Blasco Nuñez to succeed Pizarro as Viceroy, with Vaca de Castro as administrator of Peru.

Blasco enjoyed only a brief spell of power before he was defeated in a battle fought near Quito in 1545 by the dashing Gonzalo Pizarro, the only Pizarro brother to remain in Peru; as a result of this victory Gonzalo remained the undisputed master of the situation; some of the Spanish settlers even wanted to make him king. But he in turn was defeated by a new emissary of the Spanish king, Pedro de la Gasca, at Jaquijahuana, near Cuzco, in 1548 and subsequently executed. The young Diego de Almagro suffered the same fate when about to leave Cuzco to join Manco's surviving Inca rebels.

The Aftermath

Resistance, as we have seen, to the conquistadors was much greater than in many other lands that they had seized. However, the method of Spanish rule in Peru, once control had been established, followed a pattern that prevailed throughout most of their vast empire. For the average Indian, the changes were gradual. Though by this time the Spaniards must have acquired ample experience in the government of Indian lands; the inhabitants, however good their new masters' proclaimed intentions, were subjected to the same abuses.

But the direst scourge for the subjects of the newly conquered Inca Empire arose not so much from what their conquerors took, but what they brought with them in the form of hitherto unknown diseases such as measles and smallpox, against which the Native Americans had no immunity. As a result, even according to Spanish official statistics, the population of Peru fell from about 1.5 million in 1561 to 600,000 in 1796. Such statistics probably understated the reduction.

The process of depopulation was most marked on the coastal plains; for instance, Chincha, south of Lima, which had been a prosperous valley with reportedly about 40,000 inhabitants when the Spaniards arrived, was reduced to less than a thousand by the 1560s. Cieza de León lamented the terrible decline of population due to new diseases in the Ica and Nazca Valleys. But while sickness has, probably correctly, been regarded as the main cause of depopulation, profound cultural shock and an unstable political situation were also major factors.

In Peru, unlike Mexico, the demise of the old established order had been preceded by a civil war among the conquerors and, following the overthrow of the Inca Empire by wholly alien foreigners, both the staunch resistance after the Conquest and the hostilities between warring Spanish factions also took their toll; famine, resulting from the prevailing disorder, added to the horrors of war. To cite a simple example of the additional sufferings imposed upon the Indian population by fighting between Spanish factions, when Gonzalo Pizarro was advancing upon Lima, he conscripted 6000 men and women to transport his army's baggage and artillery; according to his main adversary, de la Gasca, most of these conscripts died as a result of porterage, scorched by the sun and exhausted by the weight of their loads; they were tied by chains by day and thrown into stocks by night to prevent escape.

The Spaniards' hold over the Indians was based, in Peru as in Mexico, on the system of land grants known as *encomiendas*. As early as 1529, as part of the understanding that Francisco Pizarro would undertake the conquest of Peru at his own expense, he had been granted the right to offer *encomiendas* to his people, provided that he observed certain restrictions on the use of forced labour. Thus, in effect, the King of Spain offered incentives for Spaniards not only to conquer, but to settle in conquered territories by offering them a life of privileged existence, in an age when land was the true measure of wealth among men who, unlike the future settlers of northern America, would have despised the very notion of engaging in trade, let alone in performing manual labour.

The *encomienda* granted to a Spaniard did not in itself confer land; the recipients (known as *encomenderos*) were simply entrusted with the Christian welfare of a host of Indians living within a specified territory, from whom they in turn received tribute. Hence, the *encomendero*'s reward, the incentive for him to settle in Peru, was the chance to live a life of luxury at the expense of the inhabitants of his *encomienda*. Unless rigidly controlled, the system was open to the grossest abuses. It might be one thing in Spain itself, but quite another when the control of hordes of Indians was entrusted to unprincipled individuals of alien race, who were more apt to regard them as mere beasts of burden. Unlike the previous rulers, these privileged few cared little for those with whose welfare they were charged, and in many cases exacted their tribute without ever setting eyes upon their subjects, since they were obliged to reside in a Spanish municipality, and forbidden to live within the bounds of their own domain. Virtually any soldier who had been in Cajamarca, regardless of social origin, could have an *encomienda* on condition that he remained in Peru; Pizarro tended to give the largest and best territories to his own relatives and servants and one illiterate conquistador was thus entrusted with 40,000 vassals.

The *mit'a* system of labour service was continued by the Spaniards, who turned it to their own profit. Whereas the *mitayos* conscripted for labour service were previously supported from state storehouses, the Spaniards gave them nothing in return for their labour. The most fearsome form of *mit'a* was conscription to work in the Spanish mines, where the demand for labour was vastly increased by the discovery in 1545 of the fabulous silver mines of Potosí in Bolivia, previously unknown. The silver was close to the surface and initially the Indian miners were more or less fairly treated. But by 1550 the demand for labour was so great that Potosí came to be compared to a ravenous monster, gulping down the native population. (Imported African slaves could not survive at the high altitude of the mines.) Friar Domingo de Santo Tomás was among the first to draw attention to the horrific scene in writing to the Council of the Indies in 1550: 'Some four years ago, to the complete perdition of this land, there was discovered a mouth of hell, into which a great mass of people enter every year and are sacrificed by the greed of the Spaniards to their "God". This is your silver mine called Potosí . . . the wretched Indians are sent to this mountain from every *repartamiento*. . . to be thrown by force into the mines is the condition of slaves or of men condemned to severe punishment for grave crimes.'

The higher Spanish authorities, from the king downwards, sought to protect the natives of Peru from exploitation by local residents, but the effect of their efforts was somewhat limited. As early as 1542 the Council of the Indies was established and in theory, at least, the Indians were to be protected by the New Laws, issued at Barcelona in that year. Under their provisions royal rule was extended to the provinces by the use of officials known as *corregidores*, who were instructed to punish offences against Indians as severely as if they had been inflicted upon Spaniards. But it was rare in practice for these local officials to punish the *encomenderos* and most of the population were scarcely aware of the existence of other powers, apart from their immediate masters, the *encomenderos* and the previous lords, the *curacas*.

The traditional *curacas*, or local Indian chieftains, were in effect caught between two fires. On the one hand they themselves tended to bear the brunt of Spanish cruelty, since they were thought to control much of the treasure so avidly sought by the conquerors. Atrocities against *curacas* were not infrequent; some were tortured and hanged; others were put into pits up to their waists and then pressed for gold.

But after the initial hunt for treasure, the *curacas*, far from being treated as responsible for hoarding gold, came to be regarded as a useful asset in the task of controlling their previous subjects, since the *encomenderos* were forbidden to live on their lands and therefore needed the help of these *curacas* to extract tribute. Far from being deprived of their former powers under the Inca state, many *curacas* ultimately joined the Spaniards in exploiting the local population. None the less, while some *curacas* clearly abused their newfound autonomy, others sought to protect their former subjects, and certain accounts tell of efforts by the best of them to defend their Indians from Spanish abuse.

Apart from the *encomendero* and the *curaca*, the Spaniards with whom Indians had the most direct contact were the priests; of these, while some strove to protect their flock of new converts from abuse, others did little more than add, by their claims, to the weight of tribute paid by the local population.

While ostensibly the initial purpose of the Spanish Conquest of the Indians had been their conversion and the salvation of their souls, in practice the Church as a whole had been far from united in its attitude. Long previous to the Conquest of Peru, the pro-Indian movement had found a champion in the indefatigable Bishop Bartolomé de las Casas, whose invective forced the Spanish Crown to pass a series of new laws designed, at least in theory, to protect initially the native peoples of Mexico and subsequently those of Peru.

The Spanish monarchs had been profoundly troubled by a growing debate over their moral rights to rule and conquer Indians. This debate grew ever more passionate, culminating in a gathering of ten members of the Council of the Indies and of Castilla in Valladolid in 1550. Las Casas prepared a treatise of 550 pages, which he read in seriation for five consecutive days. Notwithstanding the contrary opinions given by others, such as the humanist Juán de Sepulveda, who defended Spanish rights to rule the Indians as they thought fit, the views of las Casas tended to prevail and he continued to pour forth diatribes against misrule until his death in 1566; he even proposed that the King of Spain, for the sake of his soul's salvation, should restore all Peru to Titu Cusi, the puppet Inca ruler.

But theorizing on the moral rights of the conquerors, however well intentioned, was somewhat remote from the realities of life and social conditions of the native people of Peru and, as we have seen, there was little improvement. It was not until the arrival of the Viceroy Francisco de Toledo in 1571 that changes were made in practice. Toledo, somewhat paradoxically, sought to withdraw from circulation the writings of las Casas and displayed a certain sympathy for the natives' oppressors, the *encomenderos*; but while attempts to suppress the *encomiendas* failed, their importance tended to decline. Toledo also sought to curb the powers of the *curacas*, whom he regarded as petty tyrants. Control of the Indians was now entrusted to the *corregidores*, appointed for only a few years. Some, at least, sought to relieve their sufferings, but their efforts were often frustrated by the voracious demands of the mines for labour under conditions that failed to improve.

After the last shadow ruler, Tupac Amaru, had been executed following a mock trial, the surviving nobility by the end of the sixteenth century was increasingly assimilated and came to identify itself with the conquerors.

So marked had been the Inca impact on the core regions of their great domain that Inca traditions and customs were slow to fade and certain forms of Inca solidarity were not altogether extinguished. This simmering resentment against the Spanish overlords eventually led to an open revolt that broke out in 1737, and spread over seventeen provinces before it was ruthlessly put down. A subsequent revolt was led by a man named Santos, who took the title of Apu Inca, thus claiming to link himself with Atahualpa. Somewhat paradoxically this revolt flourished in the jungle lying beyond the confines of the former empire; the rebel 'Inca' was never captured, since he managed to retreat to the forest whenever he was pursued.

Another important uprising took place in 1780–81 and was led by a *curaca*, Gabriel Condorcanqui, who took the title of Tupac Amaru II, after the last shadow Inca, whose daughter had married Condorcanqui's great-grandfather. This was in effect a peasant revolt, which culminated in the hanging of a prominent Spanish *corregidor*. But after his initial triumph, Tupac Amaru II was captured, tortured and then executed in the main square of Cuzco.

Yet a further rebellion by Indian leaders, who claimed descent from the Incas, took place in 1815, only nine years before the battle of Ayacucho, which led to Peruvian independence from Spain.

SELECT BIBLIOGRAPHY

GENERAL

Generalized books on pre-Columbian civilizations in the Andes tend to concentrate on the brief Inca period, and say little about pre-Inca Peru.

As an exception to this one may cite *The Incas and Their Ancestors* by Michael E. Moseley (London: Thames and Hudson, 1992). Notwithstanding its title, the book deals mainly with the various pre-Inca cultures.

Equally, *Peru Before the Incas* by Edward P. Lanning (Englewood Cliffs: Prentice Hall, 1967) outlines what was already then known of the earlier cultures.

CHAPTER ONE: THE FIRST CIVILIZATIONS

Outstanding among writing on this subject is the work of Richard L. Burger, *Chavin and the Origins of Andean Civilization* (London: Thames and Hudson, 1992). In addition to giving an up-to-date account of Chavin itself, Burger offers a detailed description of the Late Preceramic and Initial Period societies, the earliest of which long preceded Chavin, once regarded as the cradle of Andean civilization.

Also of importance is the report on the Dumbarton Oaks conference on 'Early Ceremonial Architecture in the Andes' (Washington, D.C.: Dumbarton Oaks Research Library, 1985).

Richard Burger's book, cited above, contains an ample bibliography of works on the earlier cultures.

CHAPTER TWO: THE MOCHE CULTURE

The most striking work on the Moche period is *The Royal Tombs of Sipan* by Walter Alva and Christopher Donnan, first published in 1993 by the University of California at Los Angeles. Beautifully illustrated, it describes in detail these recent and sensational investigations.

The following are some of the most informative works on this period:

Benson, Elizabeth, *The Mochica, a Culture of Peru* (New York: Praeger, 1972)

Castillo, Luis Jaime, *Personas miticos, escenas y narraciones en la iconografía mochica* (Lima: Universidad Católica, 1989)

Donnan, Christopher, *Moche Art of Peru* (Los Angeles: University of California, 1978)

Hocquenghem, Anne Marie, *Iconografía mochica* (Lima: Universidad Católica, 1987)

Kirkpatrick, Sidney D., *Lords of Sipan* (New York: Henry Holt, 1992)

Moseley, Michael, *The Incas and Their Ancestors*, pp. 166–84 (London: Thames and Hudson, 1992)

Silverman, Helaine, *Cahuachi in the Ancient Nazca World* (Iowa City: University of Iowa Press, 1993)

CHAPTER THREE: NAZCA

Anthony Aveni's book is the most significant on the Nazca lines. It advances important new theories, while not totally discounting certain notions of earlier writers, even though many aspects of their research are no longer fully tenable.

Aveni, Anthony F., (ed.), *Order in the Nazca Lines?* (Philadelphia: American Philosophical Society, 1990)

Hawkins, Gerald, *Final Scientific Report for the National Geographic Society Expedition* (Cambridge, Mass.: Smithsonian Institution, 1969)

Morgan, Alexandra, 'The Master or Mother of Fishes: An Interpretation of Nazca Pottery Figurines and Their Symbolism' in *Recent Studies in Pre-Columbian Archaeology*, ed. Richard W. Keatinge, (Oxford: Bar International Series 421, 1988)

Paul, Anne, *Paracas Ritual Attire: Symbols of Authority in Ancient Peru* (Norman: University of Oklahoma Press, 1990)

Reiche, María, *Geheimnis der Wüste – Mystery on the Desert* (Stuttgart, 1968)

Reinhard, Johann, *The Nazca Lines: A New Perspective on Their Origin and Meaning* (Lima: Editorial Los Pinos, 1968)

Silverman, Helaine, *Cahuachi in the Ancient Nazca World* (Iowa City: University of Iowa Press, 1993)

CHAPTER FOUR: THE MIDDLE HORIZON

Accounts of much of the comparatively modern research of the Huari–Tiahuanaco horizon is combined in a single volume, *Huari Administrative Structure*, published in 1991 by the Dumbarton Oaks Research Library, Washington, D.C., following a round-table discussion attended by many Andean specialists.

After an initial chapter on the history of Huari studies, no less than twelve chapters by noted scholars describe the many Huari period sites, including Huari itself, Azángaro and Pikillacta. The book also makes it very clear that the later phases of Tiahuanaco were closely linked to Huari, with the site of Pucara possibly serving as a link between the two.

For earlier works on Tiahuanaco one may cite:

Ponce Sangines, C., *Nuevo perspectivo para el estudio de la expansión de la cultura tiwanaku* (La Paz: Editorial los Amigos del Libro, 1981)

Posnansky, Arthur, *Tihuanacu – The Cradle of American Man* (New York: J. J. Augustin, 1945)

CHAPTER FIVE: THE REALM OF CHIMOR

As in the case of the Middle Horizon, a wealth of information is provided in *The Northern Dynasties: Kingship and Statecraft in Chimor*, published in 1990 by the Dumbarton Oaks Research Library, edited by Michael E. Moseley and Alana Cordy Collins. This publication reproduces the information given in a previous symposium on the subject held at Dumbarton Oaks.

In an introductory article Michael E. Moseley offers a concise résumé of the history, the reported dynasties, the architecture and the art of Chimor. Of particular significance also is the description by Alan L. Kolata of the Chimu capital, Chan Chan, in Kolata, Alan L., (ed.), *Tiwanaku and Its Hinterland, Vol. 1: Agroecology, Archaeology and Paleoecology of an Andean Civilization* (Cambridge, Mass.: Smithsonian Institution, 1996).

Various contributions, particularly those of Christopher Donnan and Izumi Shimada, offer explicit but somewhat differing interpretations of the role played in Chimu history as described in the 'Anonymous History of Trujillo' and also in the work of the chronicler Cabello de Balboa. The various accounts of the conquest of Chimor by the Incas are outlined in my own book *The Incas*, pp. 132–6 (for details see the following bibliography of works on the Incas).

Among the more significant earlier works on Chimor are:

Rostworowski, María, *Curacas y sucesiones. Costa norte* (Lima: Imprenta Minerva, 1961)

Rowe, John H., *The Kingdom of Chimor* (*Acta Americana*, Vol. 6, pp. 26–59)

CHAPTERS SIX, SEVEN AND EIGHT: THE INCA PERIOD

Contemporary Works

Much has been written on the Incas. Among the significant works of recent decades I select only a few below. Nearly all have ample bibliographies, including my own book, *The Incas*, published in 1995 by the University of Colorado Press. Among other works may be cited:

Bauer, Brian S., *The Development of the Inca State* (Austin: University of Texas, 1992)

Bingham, Hiram, *Machu Picchu, a Citadel of the Incas* (New Haven: Yale University Press, 1930)

Brundage, Burr Cartwright, *Empire of the Inca* (Norman: University of Oklahoma Press, 1963)

Demarest, Arthur, *Viracocha. The Nature and Antiquity of the Andean High God* (Cambridge, Mass.: Peabody Museum Monographs, 1981)

Dillehay, Tom D., *Araucania, presente y pasado* (Santiago de Chile: Editorial Andres Bello, 1990)

Hyslop, John, *The Inca Road System* (New York: Academic Press, 1984)

Kendall, Ann, *Everyday Life of the Incas* (London: Batsford, 1973)

Métraux, Alfred, *The History of the Incas* (New York: Schocken Books, 1970)

Moseley, Michael E., *The Incas and Their Ancestors* (London: Thames and Hudson, 1992)

Murra, John V., *La Organización económica del estado Inca* (Lima: Instituto de Estudios Peruanos, 1978)

Pease, G. Y. Franklyn, *Del Tawantinsuyu a la historia del Perú* (Lima: Instituto de Estudios Peruanos, 1978)

Reinhard, Johann, *Machu Picchu: The Sacred Center* (Lima: Editorial Cultura, 1991)

Rostworowski, María de Díez, *Historia del Tawantinsuyu* (Lima: Instituto de Estudios Peruanos, 1988)

Wedin, Ake, *La Cronología de la historia incaica* (Gothenburg, Sweden: Instituto Ibero-Americano, 1963)

Zuidema, R. T., *Inca Civilization in Cuzco* (Austin: University of Texas Press, 1990)

Principal Historical Sources

Betanzos, Juán de, *Suma y narración de los Incas* (Madrid: Atlas, 1987)

Cabello de Balboa, Miguel, *Miscelánea Antártica* (Lima: Universidad de San Marcos, 1951)

Cieza de León, Pedro de, *El señorío de los Incas* (Lima: Promoción Editorial, S.A., 1973)

Garcilasco de la Vega, *El Inca. Primera parte de los Comentarios reales de los Incas* (Buenos Aires: Angel Rosenblat, 1970)

Santillán, Hernando de, *Historia de los Incas y relación de su gobierno* (Lima: Editores Técnicos, 1968)

Sarmiento de Gamboa, Pedro, *Historia de los Incas* (Buenos Aires: Editores Emece, 1943)

CHAPTER NINE: THE CONQUEST

Outstanding among works on the Spanish Conquest is the book of John Hemming, *The Conquest of the Incas* (London: Macmillan, 1970). The Spanish sources listed above also include fairly detailed but somewhat divergent accounts of the Spanish Conquest.

INDEX

Note: References in italics denote maps or illustrations.

PENGUIN ONLINE

READ MORE IN PENGUIN

In every corner of the world, on every subject under the sun, Penguin represents quality and variety – the very best in publishing today.

For complete information about books available from Penguin – including Puffins, Penguin Classics and Arkana – and how to order them, write to us at the appropriate address below. Please note that for copyright reasons the selection of books varies from country to country.

In the United Kingdom: Please write to *Dept. EP, Penguin Books Ltd, Bath Road, Harmondsworth, West Drayton, Middlesex UB7 ODA*

In the United States: Please write to *Consumer Sales, Penguin Putnam Inc., P.O. Box 12289 Dept. B, Newark, New Jersey 07101-5289.* VISA and MasterCard holders call 1-800-788-6262 to order Penguin titles

In Canada: Please write to *Penguin Books Canada Ltd, 10 Alcorn Avenue, Suite 300, Toronto, Ontario M4V 3B2*

In Australia: Please write to *Penguin Books Australia Ltd, P.O. Box 257, Ringwood, Victoria 3134*

In New Zealand: Please write to *Penguin Books (NZ) Ltd, Private Bag 102902, North Shore Mail Centre, Auckland 10*

In India: Please write to *Penguin Books India Pvt Ltd, 11 Community Centre, Panchsheel Park, New Delhi 110017*

In the Netherlands: Please write to *Penguin Books Netherlands bv, Postbus 3507, NL-1001 AH Amsterdam*

In Germany: Please write to *Penguin Books Deutschland GmbH, Metzlerstrasse 26, 60594 Frankfurt am Main*

In Spain: Please write to *Penguin Books S. A., Bravo Murillo 19, 1° B, 28015 Madrid*

In Italy: Please write to *Penguin Italia s.r.l., Via Benedetto Croce 2, 20094 Corsico, Milano*

In France: Please write to *Penguin France, Le Carré Wilson, 62 rue Benjamin Baillaud, 31500 Toulouse*

In Japan: Please write to *Penguin Books Japan Ltd, Kaneko Building, 2-3-25 Koraku, Bunkyo-Ku, Tokyo 112*

In South Africa: Please write to *Penguin Books South Africa (Pty) Ltd, Private Bag X14, Parkview, 2122 Johannesburg*

BY THE SAME AUTHOR

The Ancient Kingdoms of Mexico

This outstanding study spans four rich civilizations in ancient Mexico, from 1500 BC to the Spanish conquest soon after AD 1500:

The OLMECS, hunters and farmers who worshipped the man-jaguar and became the first great carvers in stone and jade.

The culture of TEOTIHUACAN, with its sumptuous palaces and gigantic Pyramids of the Sun and the Moon.

The TOLTEC dynasty, whose temples, wreathed with carvings of predatory beasts, serpents and warriors, testify to a new militaristic phase in Mexican history.

Writing for students, travellers and non-specialists, Nigel Davies puts these fascinating cultures into historical context. He discusses their arts, beliefs and customs, and their changing economic and political conditions, to build up a vivid picture of life in the kingdoms of ancient Mexico.

'Eloquent and interesting . . . he has a particular gift for sympathetic re-creation . . . it deserves to be a popular book' – *The Times Literary Supplement*